FASTS OF HINDU GODS AND GODDESSES:

GANESHA

J.N. Kaushik

Books For All

[A Division of D. K. Publishers Distributors (P) Ltd.]

Delhi - 110052

Sales Office:
D.K. Publishers Distributors (P) Ltd.
1, Ansari Road, Darya Ganj
New Delhi-110 002
Phone: 3261465, 3278368
Fax: 091-011-3264368

1996 Jai Narain Kaushik (b. 1935 –)
ISBN 81-7386-138-2

Laser Typeset & Published by:
BOOKS FOR ALL
[A Division of D.K. Publishers Distributors (P) Ltd.]
Regd Office: A-6, NIMRI Community Centre
Ashok Vihar Phase IV, Near Bharat Nagar
Delhi-110052
Phone: 7143353, 7430113
Fax: 091-011-7138265

Printed at:
D.K. Fine Art Press (P) Ltd., Delhi-110 052

PRINTED IN INDIA

PREFACE

India is a land of unity in diversity. Her underlying eternal force pervades in various walks of life—may it be literature, society or culture. It has a tremendous capacity to welcome, blend and tolerate various philosophies and life styles. Its deities are no exception to it. Every deity has its separate identity and still it forms part of one Supreme power.

Lord Ganesha is no exception to it. A common man accepts him as a son of Mahadeva-Parvati but some consider him as the creator of universe as well as its preserver and destroyer also.

The Elephant-faced God represents the elephant's power of wisdom and if enraged it can trample the mightiest. Its characteristics are in line with Indian power of wisdom, tolerance and to prove heavy for the enemy.

A lot of literature related to Ganesha is available in Sanskrit and to some extent in Hindi also. But a lot of folk literature is still limited to oral culture. The present work is a blended mixture of Sanskrit, Hindi and folk oral-culture presented to the Non-Hindi speaking population in India and abroad. It will be useful to the Hindi speaking people also because folk oral-culture is not accessible to everybody.

Moreover folk oral-culture is not generally approved by person of so called 'high culture' strata or of pseudoscientific temperament. Here an attempt has been made to present the rationale of each story. These time-tested stories represent certain human instincts and behaviour. In good olden days these stories were developed as a part of oral curriculum of oral-culture. Those who could not follow serious literature found consolance in these simple stories.

This work related to Ganesha has been presented in three parts:

Part-A

It contains introductory notes about Ganesha–Its meanings, reference in old literature, symbolic meanings, reasons for popularity, Ganapatya sect, family life, types of fasts, ways of Ganesha's worship etc.

Part-B

It contains twelve stories related to Ganesha's various aspects–why he is first laudible, his birth and marriage, his omnipotent and benevolent power, his penance for theft etc. These stories are very popular in Hindi speaking belt of North India including Punjab. The author heard these stories in his home village in Haryana. These stories are very popular in walled and rural area of Delhi State also. The speciality of these stories is that any one of them is related before any main story of any fast. This symbolises remembering Ganesha before starting any work.

Part-C

It contains sixteen stories connected with lunar calendar months, starting from Chaitra and ending with Purushottama month i.e., leap year. Most of these stories have their roots in Pauranic literature. It is believed that these stories were related in different ages by different narrators—Ganesha to Parvati, Shiva to Parvati, Lomas to Rishis, Krishna to Yudhishthir etc. This centuries-old tradition gives additional faith to their modern listeners.

The oral culture and folk literature is disappearing at a fast speed due to social changes. It is high time to conduct a country-wide survey of this literature and preserve it in audio and print form, otherwise we will feel poorer and sorry with the passage of time.

I am thankful to my octogenerian sister Pheemo Devi who narrated many stories repeatedly so that I could pass them down for print. I acknowledge my sincere thanks to those authors whose works I have consulted specially for Part-A and Part-C of this work.

It is hoped that apart from entertainment, these stories will appeal to human emotions and make them more humanitarian.

J.N. KAUSHIK

Contents

Part-A

Ganesha - An Introduction

GANESHA

Ganesha, the Elephant-faced God, is known as the Indian God of Wisdom. He is worshipped and invoked as first God on all religious occasions. Though generally known as the son of Shiva and Parvati by a common man, he is Creator, Preserver and Destroyer, the Supreme Brahma, the eternal spirit in the eyes of philosophers. He is Brahma, Vishnu and Rudra. He is earth, water, fire, air and ether. According to some western thinkers he has the same characteristics as Janus of the Latins.

Apart from the Elephant-faced God, "Ganesha" has many connotations. The Sanskrit word "Gana" has various meanings—a group, a body of followers or attendants, a troop of demi-gods considered as Shiva's attendants and under the special superintendence of Ganesha, an epithet of Ganesha, a sect, a series of roots or words belonging to the same rules, temperament, inner thinking and the like. The word "eesha" or "Isha" means—master or lord of powerful, supreme. So the combination of two words—"Gana" + "Isha" denote many meanings.

"Ganesha bears about one thousand names according to his acts. His most famous names are—Sumukha, Ekadanta, Kapil, Gaj Karnak, Lambodar, Vikata, Vighnanashak, Vinayaka, Dhumraketu, Ganadhyaksha, Bhalchandra, Gajanan. Some other names of Ganesha are—Siddha, Heramba, Ekakshara, Haridra-Ganapati, Dhundhi Ganapati, Singha Ganapati, Sankashtaharan Ganapati etc.

References in Old Literature

It is believed that "Ganesha" known as "Ganapati" also, is located in Vedic hymns. His story appears in Pauranic

Literature. The Ganesha Purana is devoted to describe his character in full form. It is considered that he wrote Mahabharata at the dictation of Vyasa, who requested for his services as a scribe from Brahma.

The Buddhists, who honour white elephant, is generally considered the epithet of Elephant-faced Ganesha. Mayadevi, Buddha's mother, dreamt as if white elephant descended from heaven and entered into her womb. Many of the Ashoka's inscriptions give respectful place to an Elephant. Even Buddha bears the names of "Vinayaka" and "Ganashreshtha".

Ganesha—Symbolic Meanings

The mystics ascribe their own symbolic meanings to the word "Gana" and "Ganesha". "Sat", "Chit", "Ananda", are the three "Ganas" and Ganesha is the master of all. "Prithivi", "Antriksha" and "Swarga" (earth-sky-heaven) are three "Ganas" and Ganesha is their master. According to astrologers "Devagana", "Manavgana", "Rakshashgana" (deities, man folk, demons) are three "ganas" and Ganesha is their lord. He is knows as "Ganesha" because he is beyond "Jagrat", "Swapna", "Sushupti" (awake, dream and state of sound sleep) states of mind and can see beyond them. He is Ganesha because, he bears the power of "Para", "Pashyanti" and "Madhyma".

Ganesha's Worship—Far and Nearer Places

Worshipping Ganesha is so popular that his idols in various forms have been located in the countries like Nepal, China, Turkistan, Tibet, Japan, Burma, Syam, Indonesia, Java, Bali, Borneo etc.

In India there are 21 Ganpati-Kshetras scattered in various states. Its worship is very popular in Maharashtra, Rajasthan,

Andhra, Karnataka, Kerala, Gujarat. Madhya Pradesh, Punjab, Uttar Pardesh, Bihar, Orissa, Bengal, Assam, Delhi, Haryana etc. Many temples are devoted to Vinayaka in Varanasi, Vrindavana and other religious places. Ganesha's idol can be seen in almost all the temples.

Artistic Presentation

Ganesha worship has inspired idol-makers and artists. Its idols are made from gold, silver, stone, wood, ordinary earth etc. In modern days its idols are casted out of many metallic alloys. Its idols can easily be found outside Hindu houses. They are meant for avoiding any untoward difficulty or calamity upon the family. Apart from idols it is painted in form of Swastik. A Swastik depicts its four hands. The word "OM" also represents Ganesha. The first part of the word " ॐ "depicts its protuberant belly, the middle part represents its trunk, Ardhachandra its tusk and the upper nasalised point—the laddoo. The businessmen paint Swastik on their account books and outside their business houses. The word 'OM' is given preference by the Aryasamajis, the follower of Swami Dayananda Saraswati. The Akalis, a sect of Sikha religion, also adore or respect the word "Omkar"—one God. The insertion of word "Om" in the beginning of each hymn, reminds one, of paying respect to Ganesha. The various Hindu sects accept the word "Om" as a common symbol of God (it may be Ganesha).

Reasons for Popularity

The popularity of Ganesha-worship, from rich to poor houses, can be attributed to various reasons. The knowledge seekers adore him to enhance their status because he is the God of Prudence and Policy. Both rich and poor face obstacles and difficulties. Ganesha-worship gives them confidence to cross all odds in life. Making an epithet of Ganesha is very simple. Wrap a kaccha thread around a small piece of clay and it represents Ganesha. Wrap a thread around a piece of cow-dung,it becomes Ganesha. Two pieces of grass wrapped in a thread also represent Ganesha. A "Supari" (betel nut) or turmeric piece wrapped in a thread is also a replica of Ganesha. Paint a Swastik and put some rice-grains on it. It also symbolises Ganesha. Put a "roli" (turmeric powder mixed with lime) dot and Ganesha is reflected in it. The root of Arka (swallow wart) also represents Ganesha. All these symbols show this belief that Gods live in animates as well as in inanimates.

People want to restore might and strength. Ganesha bears the quality of a warrior. One of his name is "Heramba" which means a boastful hero or one who resounds the warfield. His name "Vinayaka" means one who removes obstacles. It also denotes a terrible personality. His name "Vighnaraja" also depicts him as impediment remover. His war-like spirit is reflected in the weapons he bears in his hands—Parsha, Trishul, Asi, Ankusha, Pasha and Naag.

Farmers adore him because his elephant-face represents Indra—the god of rain. India is a land of farm growers. Ganesha overrides or controls mouse which harms the harvests.

The business community adopts him because his belly is like Kuber, the god of wealth. The difference between the two is that Kuber's movement is almost stand-still while Ganesha moves faster.

Moreover Ganesha is "Mangalkari"—auspicious or pleasure bestower and everybody yearns for it. Due to his intellectual capacity he is remembered before all gods. Every one desires to be respected first of all. Ganesha is considered as best writer also. Writing Ganesha in the beginning is to pay tribute to the best writer.

People bow before him because he bears numerous incarnations. Some of his well known incarnations are—Vakratunda, Ekdanta, Mahodara, Gajanana, Lambodara, Vikata, Vighnaraja, Dhumra Varna. During these incarnations he controlled, and vanished demons who represent proudness, attachment, anger, sex etc.

Creature-Faces Gods

Many gods are incarnated as bearing the face or body of creatures or animals of lowest organisation such as—Matsya, Kurma, Varaha, Narsimgha, Hayagreeva. Ganesha, the Elephant-faced god, commands the highest respect among all.

Ganapatya Sect

The followers of Ganesha are known as Ganapatya. There are other four famous sects among the Hindu - Vaishnava (Worshipper of Vishnu), Shaiva (Worshipper of Shiva), Shakta (Worshipper of Shakti), Saura (Worshipper of Sun). Ganapatya assumes important place among these five sects.

Ganapatya sect considers and remembers Ganesha as Para-Brhama or the Supreme Power. This sect has six-sub-sects. These sub-sects are:

1. Maha Ganapati
2. Haridra Ganapati
3. Uchchista Ganapati
4. Heramba Ganapati
5. Swarana Ganapati, and
6. Sanatan Ganapati

After a general background about Ganesha it will be proper to describe his other interesting aspects like birth, parentage, bodily aspects and the like.

Birth

Ganesha is the son of Shiva and Parvati or of Parvati only. He is called "Dwimatur" because he was brought up by river Ganges also. His birth story has been narrated in various Puranas and with somewhat difference. Each story has its own symbolic meanings. According to Brahma Vaivarta Purana, Parvati married Shiva but was issueless for a long period as Shiva was in his "Samadhi." She worshipped Vishnu from thirteenth day of the bright fortnight of Magha and continued it for a year. She observed a life of inward purity. Sanat Kumar was her directing priest on the bank of the Ganges. When her reward was delayed, she was plunged in grief. Aakaashwani (Viewless Voice) told her to go to her apartment where she would find a son, who is the lord of Goloka or Krishna. This deity has assumed the semblance of her son as a recompense for her devotion.

All the gods came to see her son and to congratulate Shiva and Parvati. But Shani, the planet Saturn, kept his eyes fastly fixed on the ground. Parvati asked him the reason. Shani told that due to some curse if he sees, her son would be destroyed. Parvati gave him permission without any regard to the story. Shani peeped out. Ganesha and the child's head was severed from his body and flew away to the heaven of Krishna.

Durga took the headless trunk in her arms, and cast herself weeping on the ground. Vishnu, who mounted Garuda, flew to Pushpbhadra, where he found an elephant asleep. He took off his head and clapped it on the body of Ganesha. Ganesha came back to life.

The same Purana gave some other version of Ganesha's head. Once Shiva offended with Aditya (the sun), slew him and although he restored him to life, incurred the wrath of sage Kashyapa, who doomed his (Shiva's) son to lose his head. The elephant whose head was placed upon Ganesha's body was Indra's elephant.

Matsya Purana gives a different story about Ganesha's birth. When Parvati was bathing, she took the oil and ointments used at the bath. She formed them into the figure of a man. She gave it life by sprinkling water of the Ganges. This figure had a head of an elephant. Ganesha still bears that head.

According to Shiva Purana Ganesha sprang from the scurf of Parvati's body. Parvati placed him at her door to prevent intrusion. When she was bathing, Shiva came at that moment and tried to enter the home. Ganesha prevented him and a struggle ensued. Shiva cut off Ganesha's head. When Parvati came out, she wept to see her son without head. Shiva ordered the first head that would be found, to be brought to him. This happened to be an elephant's. Shiva fitted it to the headless trunk and Ganesha became alive.

Varaha Purana describes Ganesha's birth story in a different way. It states that only Shiva produced Ganesha by his will. The story says that once gods wanted to accomplish good deeds. They desired that no difficulty may occur in their deeds. They requested Shiva to create such a mighty being. Shiva looked at Parvati and from the splendour of his countenance there sprang into existence a youth, shedding radiance and He was Ganesha. Parvati felt jealous of his beauty and in an enraged state of mind said that he should assume an elephant's head and a large belly to vanish his beauty. Shiva named him Ganesha.

In folk tales Ganesha's birth has taken a human touch. Parvati produced Ganesha out of "Ubatana," a paste for smearing the body. He asked her son to stand at the gate as a door keeper. Shiva returned after a long period of his meditation. The boy at the door introduced him as Parvati's son. He did not allow Shiva to enter the home as his mother was bathing. Shiva felt offended. He thought how Parvati can produce a child without his union. He took it a case of adultery and beheaded the boy. Parvati related him the story as how she produced Ganesha out of her heavenly power to guard her in Shiva's absence. Shiva was sorry for his act. He said, "Bring the head of any being whose mother is not sleeping face to face with her offspring." Incidentally, a female elephant was sleeping in opposite posture along with it's calf. In a way the calf was not under the protection of its mother. It was beheaded easily and its head was put on Ganesha's body. Since then Ganesha became Elephant-faced being. The female elephants whose calf's head is born by Ganesha, is known as his second mother.

Ekadanta or Single Tusk

Ganesha is shown with a broken tusk or with a single tusk behind his trunk. That is why he is known as Ekadanta. There is an interesting story connected with his broken tusk. Parshurama, an incarnation of Vishnu, was favourite disciple of Shiva. He presented him Parsha or axe which he bears with his name also. Once he went to Kailasha to see Shiva. On arriving at his inner palace he was stopped by Ganesha who was guarding his father and mother who were inside the palace. Parshurama felt offended and tried to enter forcibly. After a long dialogue the two came to blows. Ganesha seized Parshurama in his trunk and left him sick and senseless. When he came to his senses, he threw his axe on Ganesha's tusk. Ganesha recognised the weapon given by his father to

Parshurama. So he received it with all humility upon his tusk which was immediately severed and hence Ganesha lost one tusk. Parvati was enraged to see her son with one tusk. She thought of cursing Parshurama for defacing her son. But soon Krishna appeared on the scene and pacified her anger. This result of his combat with Parshurama was in consequence of a curse pronounced upon him by the sage Tulsi, with whom he had quarrelled. (so Tulsi is not offered to Ganesha).

According to other story once Gajasura, a great demon, challenged Ganesha and both come to blows. Gajasura gave a fatal blow on Ganesha's right tusk and so it was broken. Gajasura tried to evade Ganesha by transforming himself as a mouse but Ganesha recognised him and made him his vehicle permanently.

Other parts of his body are also symbolic of certain qualities. Small eyes suggest that one should overlook other's abuses. Large ears suggest that one should be careful about environmental happenings. His pot like belly suggests the power of tolerance though one may be provoked by taunts. An interesting story about his extended belly is that when he was sucking Parvati's breast, he sucked too much milk out of jealousy. Skand remained without milk.

Ganesha's Vehicles

Ganesha's famous vehicle is mouse but in different ages he adores separate vehicles. In "Satyuga" he is called Vinayaka and adores "Simgha" or lion.

In "Tretayuga" he is known as Mayureshwar and rides Mayur or Peacock.

In "Dwapar Yuga" he bears the name of Gajanana and he rides Mushaka or Mouse. At present we worship him as a mouse rider though it is Kaliyuga.

In Kaliyuga he is known as Dhumraketu and rides a horse. He bears two hands to destroy "Mlechha."

Originally, as another story says, mouse was used by Shiva and later on he passed it on to Ganesha. The mouse has been symbolised in various ways. Firstly, it represents spirit of sex which disturbs every creature. One who can control it become Ganapati or the ruler. Secondly, evil spirits remain hidden in darkness like a mouse and play hidden games. Their control helps human beings for self evolution. Thirdly, a mouse represents a logical mind which analyses small aspects by making them threadbare. One who controls logical mind for human benefit gets due regards.

God's vehicles possess godly powers and so they are worshipped like Gods. That is why we have special regard to elephant, peacock, lion etc. The environmentalists can explore this aspect for protecting animals.

Ganesha's Weapons

Every incarnation possesses certain weapons to curb the evil forces. These weapons are divine weapons bestowed by other gods as a help to wipe out the obstacles on his way. Ganesha is the god of remover of all obstacles and impediments. He had to fight many demons to bring peace and tranquillity in the society.

Generally there are ten main weapons—Vajra, Shakti, Danda, Khadga, Pasha, Ankusha, Gada, Trishula, Padma and Chakra. Shakti and Gada are feminine genders, Chakra and Padma are neutral genders, while all the remaining are masculine genders. Apart from the above ten weapons, Ganesha possessed other articles like Dhwaja, Baan, Dhanusha, Kamandala, Ikshudanda, Danta, Mudgara etc., as per requirement from time to time. Ganesha killed many demons like Dhumraksha, Narkantaka, Devantaka with these weapons to bring peace in his kingdom.

It is said that Ganesha got many weapons when he went out for begging after Yajnyopaveeta (wearing of sacred thread) ceremony. Varuna gave him Pasha, Shankar donated Trishula, Parshurama's mother Renuka gave Parshu. All these gods gave him enough training to use those weapons in needy moments.

Ganesha's Family

Brother

Swami Kartikeya is considered as his elder brother. But in race competition around the world Ganesha won the race. The symbol behind this defeat is that Ganesha is the spiritual power while Kartikeya represents physical power of Parvati. Ganesha represents faith while Kartikeya is symbol of human efforts or exertion. Spiritual power has always been upper hand as compared to physical power.

Wives

Riddhi - Siddhi and Buddhi are Ganesha's two wives. One can possess these powers only when one possesses power to overrule evil spirits which always stand as hurdles.

Sons

Symbolically Ganesha has two sons—Kshema and Laabha. The former means prosperous and the later profit. An ordinary person cannot possess these wordly possessions. One who attains "Shivatva" can be proud of these treasures.

Temples Decorum

Each temple, where Ganesha's idol is ordained, follow a proper system for his decorum. Its idol is surrounded by eight sub-idols in the following order:-

1. Gajakarna - to its left.
2. Siddhi - to its right.
3. Gauri - to its North.
4. Buddhi - to its East ward.
5. Balachandra - to its South East.
6. Saraswati - to its North.
7. Kuber - West ward.
8. Dhoomketu - hindward.

All the eight Dwarapals or door keepers outside its temples are dwarfs, bearing different weapons. These Dawarpals are – Avighna-Vighnaraja (East) Suraktra-Balwan (South) Gajakarna-Gokarna (West) Susaumya-Subhdayaka (North).

History of Fasts

It will be proper to say some words about the history of fasts with special references to Ganesha. History of fasts in India can be traced out from Vedic period. It permeates throughout Pauranic period. There are references of fasts in the Ramayana and the Mahabharata.

In literature there are two words generally used for fasts— "Upvasa" and "Vrata". "Upavasa" generally means to go without meal. The reasons for forgoing the meals can be varied. One type of "Upavasa" is not to take food due to illness. It is called "Langhan." These days we generally hear people resorting to "Upavasa" or "Anasana" due to political reasons. Sometimes non-availability of food amounts to compulsory fast. But these days not to take food willingly due to religious reasons is called "Upavasa" or "Vrata". The word

"Vrata" is more appropriate for fast because its main stress is to resolve, pacca determination (not to take meal).

In Vedic literature we found a reference to "Agni Upasana Vrata". Agni Upasana Vrata and the like mere meant for avoiding pain and attaining happiness. The "Vrata" was considered the simplest way for attaining happiness by avoiding sinful deeds and performing pious acts. By avoiding food or taking it in small quantity keeps one fit—mentally as well as physically. It promotes the power of concentration also.

In Vedic times fasts were few and simple. But in Pauranic times their number increased and several concessions and alternatives were added to them.

Types of Fasts

The fasts can be categorised under certain categories—Timings, aims, sex etc. Mahavrata continues for 16 years whereas Vedavrata and Dhwaja Vrata can continue for 12 years. Panchmahabhuta Vrata may end in one year while Arandhuti Vrata is observed in Vasanta or spring only.

According to aims the Vratas are of three types—

1. *Nitya Vrata:* to speak the truth, to be chaste, to control passion, to avoid anger, not to use vulgar language, not to speak ill of others.

2. *Naimitika:* These Vratas are connected with certain causes or occasions. For example it may be due to some "Pataka" or sin committed. Chandrayana Vrata can be placed under this category.

3. *Kamya:* Fasts observed to fulfil some desire, wish, to attain some object. For example desire to have a son, to regain lost property, to win litigation, to finish enemies etc., are

common desires these days. Most of the fasts fall under this category.

Sexwise Fasts

Some of the fasts are meant for male and others are for females only. Some of them can be observed by both the sexes. For example Shravana Purnima Vrata is for male and Haritalika, Karkchaturthi, Ahoi fasts are observed by females. Some of the fasts can be observed by married and un-widowed while others by unmarried and unwidowed also. The Vratas like Ekadasi and Kanyadaan can be observed by couples.

Monthwise Fasts

Certain fasts are observed in certain months on certain "tithis" or dates and those too in certain "Naxatras" and "Karnas". For example Nirjala Ekadashi Vrata is observed in the month of Jyeshtha and Maha Shivaratri in Falguna.

Chastity During Fasts

Certain rules, rites and customs are observed during fast days. For example - to get early in the morning, taking bath, uttering prayers, to be polite, avoid sleep during day, taking simple meal at appointed time, avoiding non-vegetarian food, wine and sex, donations according to one's capacity etc. The main aim is to elevate oneself in each and every behaviour because the belief is that gods avoid the company of ill character fellows. One who observes fasts can please her or his gods, Rishis, Pitras and fellow beings. The psychological background of the fasts is to make a man habitual of good practices. He or she may practise these habits weekly, fortnightly or on certain marked occasions. A fast undertaken with full faith can save one's present life and paves way for the coming births.

In Jain Dharma also fasts like Ahimsa, Asteya keep one to shed bad deeds and follow chaste path. It has been observed that even non vegetarian society generally avoid meat and resort to vegetarian food during fasting days.

Fasts Related to Ganesha

The fasts related to Ganesha are observed on 4th day of the Indian lunar Calendar every month. Bhadrapada Shukla Chaturthi, the sixth month of Vikram Samvata, is known as Ganesha's birth day. This day is celebrated with fret and fervour in India. Usually all the 4th days of the black half fortnight or Krishan Paksha are observed as Ganesha Chaturthi days. But in the month of Bhadrapada and Magha, 4th day of the bright half fortnight assumes special importance.

As stated earlier Ganesha, the Elephant-Faced god, represents Indra and is worshipped by one and all, as first god on all auspicious occasions.

Ganesha—A Symbol of National Unity

Elephant-faced Ganesha represents the Indian way of thinking. In most of the cases the elephant remains calm and cool as the proverb goes—it does not care for barking dogs. But if enraged it can devastate everything. Delhi, the seat of Pandavas, selected elephant as its symbol of wisdom and might and it still stands a symbol or insignia of University of Delhi.

During our struggle against foreign rule, Lokamanya Tilak reviewed the tradition of celebrating Ganesha Chaturthi as a symbol of National unity in 1893 in Pune. All the communities, regardless of caste and creed joined this movement. Even our Muslim brethren joined this festival. This festival is celebrated till date. It also provides rich opportunity to our artisans and artists who prepare Ganesha's model most artistically.

Way of Ganesha's Worship

The way of worshipping Ganesha for a common man is very easy. Wrap a thread around a kachcha pebble. Sprinkle fresh water and say "Shri Ganeshaya Namaha" (I bow before Ganesha). If some one has time, knowledge, resources, he or she can worship him by adopting "Shodashaupcharas" or sixteen rituals. They are as under:-

1. Asana—seat for worshipping
2. Swagatam—welcome sermons
3. Arghya—libation
4. Achmana—sipping of water as ceremony
5. Madhuparka
6. Snana—offering sacred baths
7. Vastrabharana—offering clothes
8. Yajnopavita—offering sacred thread (Janeoo)
9. Chandana—offering Sandal
10. Pushpa—offering flowers
11. Dhup—to incense
12. Deep—offering lighted earthen lamp
13. Naivedya—oblation
14. Tambol—offering betel leaf
15. Parikrama—to go around as a mark of respect
16. Vandana—obeisance

One of Ganesha's name is "Moda" or Modaka Priya. "Moda" means "laddoo." Laddoos are the special offerings. One may offer laddoos, distribute laddoos in Ganesha's name or eat laddoos at the time of breaking fast. One can donate

Ganesha's metallic or other types of Ganesha's idols. One can offer food to the priests or to the deserving poors.

The observer of Ganesha's fast should take simple meal only once, after looking the rising moon and offering water to it. On Bhadrapada Chaturthi, the 4th day of the bright half fortnight, seeing moon is prohibited because it invites false blemish. On this day Ganesha worship is arranged in the afternoon.

Part - B

General Stories Related To Lord Ganesha

1

Ganesha - The First Laudible God

(This story is related to Ganeshà Chaturthi, the 4th day of every fortnight, according to Indian lunar Calendar month. Before telling the main story this story is considered as a starter story.

The purpose of this story, apart from religious belief seems that every one should pay first and foremost regard to one's parents. In parents resides the replica of universe, earth and all the holy pilgrimages. Moreover, one should not be boastful. It also reminds us to know about our real destination hundred times before we proceed.)

Once a big calamity befell upon the gods. They went to Lord Shiva, the God of Gods. They related their story of grief to Lord Shiva. Lord Shiva gave them a patient hearing.

Swami Kartikeya and Ganesha, Shiva's two sons were seated with him. Lord Shiva looked towards them and smiled. He said, "One who performs this work will be worshipped first among all gods. Who is prepared for this job?"

Swami Kartikeya, the eldest son of the Lord Shiva, said, "I am the supreme commander of god's army. Who else deserves this high assignment? Assign this job to me only and confer this honour upon me."

Lord Shiva looked towards Ganesha. Ganesha said, "I do not need any high degree. I believe in doing work. I am always at your command like an ordinary soldier. Confer any rank to Swami Kartikeya and assign the work to me."

Lord Shiva smiled on Ganesha's politeness and said, "O my dear sons, both of you make three rounds around the earth. Whosoever comes first will be worshipped first among all gods."

Swami Kartikeya saddled on the peacock back and flew for the journey around the earth. The peacock flew over the earth at an unimaginable speed.

Ganesha hinted the mouse to be ready for a ride. The mouse moved its tail as a signal for readiness. He rode on the rat. Ganesha had firm belief that who can be greater than the parents. Even their hearts are larger than the entire earth. He made three rounds around his mother, the goddess Parvati and father Shiva. He bowed before them and sat in their feet.

On the other hand Swami Kartikeya was flying at a high speed. Whatever land he covered he spotted the signs of mouse paws ahead of him. He thought as if he was running a losing competition. He would not win the title of being worshipped first among gods.

Swami Kartikeya returned to his parents after completing three rounds around the earth. He found that Ganesha was sitting calm and cool at their feet.

Lord Shiva said, "My dear Kartikeya, you have lost the competition. Ganesha is the winner."

Swami Kartikeya said, "Respected father, I have made three successful rounds around the earth. Ganesha is sitting here calm and cool. How can he be a winner? How can a mouse run faster than a peacock?"

Lord Shiva said, " Better ask this question from Ganesha."

Kartikeya challenged Ganesha and said, "How could you complete three rounds around the earth riding over a slow paced mouse?"

"I did not need that," said Ganesha.

"Then how could you be the winner?" asked Kartikeya.

Ganesha said, "My dear elder brother, the entire earth resides in mother's soul and the Dharma rests with the father. Why should I stumble on rough earth when I can easily make rounds around my parents. People unnecessarily stumble for pilgrimages. Better to serve our parents and get their blessings instead of undertaking arduous journey for sacred places. I made three rounds around my parents and they have already blessed me."

Lord Shiva heard Ganesha's version and said, "O my little son, really you deserve to be worshipped first among all gods. You accompany the gods and remove their sufferings.

Ganesha accompanied the gods and fulfilled their desires.

2

LORD GANESHA'S BIRTH STORY

(The present story is related to Lord Ganesha's birth. The story depicts a woman's fear towards labour pains and still her inner tender desire for becoming a mother, a natural womanly urge.)

Once there was a Himalayan king. His name was Himachal. He had two daughters. He named them Parvatı and Gauran. He loved them very much.

Once the members of the family were talking about their fortunes. King Himachal said to Gauran, "Who is your feeder?"

The girl said, "O my beloved father, you are my feeder."

The King was pleased to hear her reply. The king put the same question to Parvati. Parvati said, "How a father can be my feeder My feeder is my own fortune."

The king was annoyed by her answer. He called for a Brahman and said, "Search out a beautiful prince for Gauran. She is my deserving daughter. And let Parvati be married to some beggar. She is very haughty. She is proud of her own fortune."

The Brahman searched a beautiful prince for Gauran. The king married Gauran with a prince. He gave a big bounty in her marriage.

The Brahman saw an ordinary old beggar in the street. He proposed Parvati's marriage with that beggar. The king Himachal agreed. He gave Parvati to the old beggar. He made no other donation in the marriage.

Parvati left her father's house happily. On her way to his husband's house she realised that the old beggar was no one else but Lord Shiva himself. Parvati became happy to know the revelation.

When Parvati entered her husband's territory, she found that the grass under her each step withered away. Lord Shiva called an astrologer to know the fact. The astrologer said, "Parvati used to keep fast in the name of Aasha Bhagwati along with her sister-in-law. If Parvati visits her parents, she would be free from this sin."

Lord Shiva agreed to visit his father-in-law's house. He started his journey with all the kingly pomp and show. All of them visited their parents and performed the religious rites of the fasts on their accomplishment.

On her wayback Parvati saw a crowd. She wanted to know the cause of the gathering. Shiva told her that a mare is about to deliver a calf. She is in trouble and making labour to free herself from the pains. Parvati said, "O my Lord, delivery is the greatest problem attached to females. Cannot they be freed from this trouble? You do me a favour. Cannot you make me a barren lady. I desire to be free from labour pain."

Lord Shiva smiled and said, "Do not challenge nature. Every female desires to be a mother sooner or later. Do not ask for this boon."

Shiva and Parvati continued their journey. Parvati again noticed a crowd. She wanted to know the cause of that crowd. Lord Shiva said "a woman is about to deliver a child. She is suffering from labour pains. Some ladies are trying to free her from the pains."

Parvati again said to Lord Shiva, "O Lord Shiva, delivery is the great problem attached to female. . . . Cannot you make me a barren lady. . . . "

Lord Shiva smiled and repeated the same words. Parvati was so much moved by seeing the labour pains that she repeatedly requested Lord Shiva to make her free from the burden of delivering the child. Lord Shiva agreed and blessed her for the fulfilment of her desire for not delivering a baby.

They met Gauran on their way. She was passing a very poor and miserable life. When Shiva and Parvati reached their home her parents could not recognise them. They could not believe their eyes that Parvati was having a luxurious life. She said to Himachal, "O my dear father, my feeder is my own fortune."

Parvati said to her sister-in-law, "I am here to accomplish my fast observed in the name of Aasha Bhagwati. I do not see sufficient arrangement for the same."

Lord Shiva sensed the whole situation and he made all the necessary arrangements for the accomplishment of Parvati's fasts.

When Parvati started her return journey with Shiva she spotted a beautiful colt playing with the mare. The colt was alert and attractive. Parvati said, "Which is that animal my Lord?"

Lord Shiva said, "You saw a mare in trouble last time. That mare has given birth to this colt. See its beauty. No pain, no gain."

Parvati smiled and marched after Lord Shiva. Parvati saw a beautiful young child playing in the lap of a lady. She said, "who is that beautiful child playing in the lap of his mother?"

Lord Shiva said, "You saw a lady undergoing labour pains last time. The lady has given birth to this child. No pain,no gain."

Parvati smiled and said, "I too want a child in my lap. I want to become a mother."

Lord Shiva said, "How can you deliver a child? You wanted to live as a barren lady. I have blessed you that boon. You cannot deliver a baby. I do not take back my words."

The motherly tender desire began to trouble Parvati. She too wanted to lull a baby in her lap. She wanted to kiss the tender lips of a new born baby. She wanted to listen praise-songs of the baby in child-bed. She wanted to worship village well amidst merry songs. So many imaginations were marred by the boon.

She caught hold of Lord Shiva's feet and begged pardon for shirking from the labour pains. Lord Shiva was pleased with her imploration. He took out a magic purse and made a mixture of mud with other articles. He raised a small baby out of the filth and handed over it to Parvati. She named the baby as Ganesha.

3
VINAYAKA'S MARRIAGE

(This story suggests that one should not make fun or ignore an ugly looking creature or one's food habits. Even this sort of creature can create enormous trouble, if disturbed unnecessarily.)

Once Lord Vishnu decided for a marriage. He selected goddess Lakshmi as a marriage companion. A grand marriage party was arranged for the wedding. Lord Vishnu invited all the gods for accompanying him for the wedding.

One of the gods said, "It is a happy occasion for get-together of all the gods. We are missing Lord Ganesha in the party. How an auspicious work can be completed without him. I doubt some calamity may fall on us."

Lord Vishnu smiled and said, "Ganesha's features are very clumsy. His nose resembles with elephant-calf's trunk. His ears are like winnowing baskets. His forehead is flat. His eyes are small like pills. His feet are like mortar of stone. He has a pot belly. Women and children from my father-in-law's city will laugh at him.

"Moreover his diet is very strange. He takes one maund of black gram, quarter and one maund of rice and much of ghee as his breakfast. He will take a long time in taking his meal. Members of the wedding party would have to wait for him. The women from my father-in-law's house will sing sarcastic songs about his diet. He may become angry and may spoil cheerful atmosphere."

Lord Ganesha was appointed as a homeguard in the absence of the marriage party. Ganesha accepted the offer without hesitation. The marriage party left for the bride's house with full pomp and show. Lord Vishnu was seated in a golden chariot. His chariot was driven by twelve horses at a high speed.

Lord Ganesha was all alone at the house. Narada happened to come to that way. Narada said, "O Lord Ganesha, why are you all alone here? Where are the other members of your family?"

Lord Ganesha said, "They are gone out for a marriage. Lord Vishnu wants to wed Lakshmi."

"But did you not accompany them?" said Narada.

"They had faith in me. They have kept me on guard," said Lord Ganesha.

Narada said, "You have been cheated by Lord Vishnu. You are an innocent boy. They have left you behind because your physical features are clumsy."

"Is it so?" said Ganesha.

"Yes, the story is quite otherwise," said Narada.

"What should I do now? I want to teach Vishnu a lesson," said Ganesha.

Narada said, "The solution is very simple. You are all powerful. Ask your mouse force to make the earth hollow. Vishnu's chariot would be struck in deep ditches. You should ask about your own marriage before Vishnu's wedding."

Lord Ganesha ordered his mice force to follow the marriage party and make the path hollow. In the twinkling of an eye the mice force reached the spot and hollowed the earth.

Vishnu's wedding chariot got stuck into a deep ditch. The horses tried their best to pull out the chariot but all in vain.

The members of the marriage procession were much worried. The pandit feared that auspicious moment set for the wedding may pass. All of them whispered. They decided to call a carpenter to prepare another chariot for Lord Vishnu.

The carpenter reached the spot. Before starting his work he remembered and recalled Lord Ganesha's name. All the members of the marriage party were surprised. One of the members said, "Is Lord Ganesha so powerful that you remember his name? Is he more powerful than Lord Vishnu?"

"Certainly," said the carpenter.

"How," said one of the gods.

The carpenter said, "Lord Ganesha has stopped Vishnu's marriage chariot."

"But Ganesha is guarding the home. He is not here," said another god.

"Lord Ganesha is omnipresent. Over his bidding his mice-force has hollowed down the path. I can make a light chariot. It will also get stuck into the earth. The marriage party should return. Make home in Lord Ganesha. No marriage can be performed before his worship," said the carpenter.

All the gods were at their wits end. The marriage party returned to accompany Lord Ganesha. Lord Vishnu tendered his unqualified apology and tried to persuade him to join the marriage party.

Lord Ganesha said, " I will join your marriage party after my own marriage. I want to marry Riddhi-Siddhi."

All the gods joined Lord Ganesha's wedding with Riddhi-Siddhi. Lord Ganesha joined Lord Vishnu's marriage.

4

The Omnipotent Lord Ganesha

(The story manifests the magic power of Gods. It also reveals that taking meal before offering it to a guest is a discourteous act.)

Once Lord Ganesha had a small earthen pot and a small earthen cup. The pot was full of milk and the cup with uncooked rice. He wandered here and there requesting everybody to prepare kheer dish for him. Everybody laughed his childlike behaviour.

An old lady saw him. She felt pity and said, "I shall prepare a dish (Kheer) for you."

Lord Ganesha said, "Dear old mother, bring a large brass disc and a big brass pitcher."

The old lady said, "I am very poor. I do not possess big utensils."

Lord Ganesh said, "Please go inside and you shall find these utensils in your kitchen."

The lady went inside and found the utensils. Lord Ganesha filled the shallow–large disc with rice and the pitcher with milk.

Lord Ganesha said, "You prepare the dish. I shall return soon to eat it."

The old lady started cooking the dish (Kheer). The milk began to overflow from the pot.

The old lady's daughter-in-law said, "The milk is over flowing. Why do you not put some preparation in my plate."

The old lady said, "Lord Ganesha is about to return. He will consider our act as bad. He will be annoyed for touching the dish before presenting it to him."

The daughter-in-law said, "Ganesha is not omnipresent. He will not look our act."

The old lady agreed and put some preparation in her disc. The daughter-in-law hid herself behind a door and began to eat. The old woman sat outside the door as a guard.

Soon after Lord Ganesha returned. The old lady said, "O dear son, enjoy the dish."

Lord Ganesha said, "O old mother, you take it yourself. Ask your family members to enjoy it. You ask one and all to join this feast. I tasted this dish when you served it to your daughter-in-law. Your daughter-in-law is still sipping it."

The old lady felt guilty. She had no other way except to distribute it to the neighbours. She served it to one and all but the pot could not be emptied. It was late evening. The old lady got tired.

She washed the pot in the river. To her great surprise the water turned into milk.

Once a king came there for hunting. He felt thirsty. He went to the river. He was surprised to see the milk-river. He said to his courtiers, "Search out the person who has turned water river into milky one."

People told the courtiers, "They saw an old lady. She was distributing 'Kheer' dish to everybody. She came to riverside for washing the pot. She has done this magic."

The king sent for the old lady. The old lady presented herself before the king. She was trembling. The old lady related the whole story of Lord Ganesha to the King. The King was highly pleased to listen the story.

5

LORD GANESHA'S PENANCE

(The story reveals that the farmers' field is an open treasure. Even taking few grains without his permission is an act of theft. One can shed his sin only by penance.)

Once Lord Ganesha was passing through the fields riding on the rat-driven cart. The crop was about to ripe. Lord Ganesha could not help tasting some fresh green grains. As he tasted the grains, the owner of the field happened to come there. Ganesha saw the landlord and felt guilty of theft. He decided to undergo some penance.

Ganesha went to the owner of the field. He offered his free service to the landlord. The landlord agreed to avail of his services. Ganesha introduced himself as Ganesha. The landlord liked his name.

One day landlord's wife returned from the fields after nature call. She was washing her hands with ash of the hearth. Ganesha noted it. He caught her hand immediately. The lady was surprised at his unusual behaviour. She rebuked him. Ganesha said, "I cannot tolerate washing hands with ash after nature call. The ash is dead earth. Wash your hands with newly dug earth."

The lady complained against Ganesha's behaviour to her husband. The landlord approved Ganesha's good gesture and ignored his wife's complaint. Ganesha believed that washing hands with ash deprives one of Riddhi and Siddhi.

Once it was the occasion of the holy Ganges bath. The landlord was preoccupied with some business work. He asked Ganesha to accompany his wife to the Ganges. Ganesha agreed.

The landlord's wife sat on the bank side to take her bath. The water on the bank was very dirty. So many people had made the water dirty. Ganesha took her hand and dragged her to the deep water. The lady resented and said, "Don't you feel ashamed by catching my hand publicly and dragging me to deep water?"

Ganesha said, "Water on the bank side is muddy. People have made it impure. You must take your bath in fresh water. You will get reward in the next birth by taking bath in fresh water."

The lady returned and made complaint against Ganesha's behaviour. Ganesha related the whole incident. The landlord did not mind Ganesha's behaviour; rather he praised his gesture.

Once the landlord arranged a Yajna ceremony at his house. He asked Ganesha to call his wife to join the ceremony. Ganesha went to the landlord's wife. Ganesha tore the lady's blouse. She was shocked at Ganesha's advancement. She was highly enraged and rebuked Ganesha.

Ganesha did not mind. He said, "Today is an auspicious day. You are going to join a holy ceremony. How can you wear black clothes. Wear red blouse."

The lady went inside and changed the blouse. The lady told her husband about Ganesha's unwanted behaviour. Ganesha gave his own explanation. The landlord did not mind his behaviour; rather he praised Ganesha's gesture.

The landlord sat for performing the ceremony. The pandit said, "I have forgotten to bring Ganesha's idol. How can we start the ceremony without worshipping Ganesha."

Ganesha said, "Do not worry. Take me as Ganesha. The goddess will fulfil your desire." The landlord became angry and said, "I have rationalised your behaviour with my wife. You have crossed all limits. You make fun of me at the auspicious moment."

Ganesha said, "I am not cutting jokes with you." He turned himself into a real Ganesha. The landlord and his wife offered him worship. At the end of the worship Lord Ganesha disappeared from the scene.

They were surprised to see all that happened. They felt sorry for ordering Lord Ganesha for domestic jobs. Ganesha appeared in the landlord's dream and said, "Do not feel sorry for your behaviour towards me. I did all this as a penance. Once I tasted some grains from your field. I felt guilty of being a thief. I decided to serve you as a penance."

The landlord became still richer and he too made donations as a penance.

6

A Frog Couple And Ganesha

(This story tells that one should not make fun of other's faith. Haughty male generally suffers for his proud behaviour.)

Once there lived a frog couple. The female frog used to get up early in the morning to have a holy dip. She always uttered prayers in the name of Lord Ganesha.

Once the male frog became angry and gave her a beating. He said, "Why do you utter other man's name everyday instead of mine."

The female frog said, "My Lord, excuse me for my folly. Hence onward I shall utter my prayer in your name alone and not in anybody else's name."

Next day she got up early in the morning. She had a pious bath. The male frog noted her activities. The female frog was dipping again and again. She was uttering the name of her male companion i.e., frog. The frog was happy.

A washerman happened to come at that time. He dipped his pitcher in the water. Incidentally, the frog couple was caged in the pitcher.

The washerman put the pitcher on the hearth. He lit up the fire from below. The water became hotter and hotter. Both of them felt very uneasy due to heat.

The male frog said to his female companion, "Dear frog, we never faced such a danger. We are badly in hot water. Utter the name of your Lord you used to utter in your prayers."

The female frog said, "My Lord, I remember your beating. I shall not utter anybody else's name. I shall utter your name alone."

The male frog said, "Dear companion, our life is in danger. Please utter the same name. We are about to perish. The death is before us."

The female frog said, "I used to utter my prayers in the name of Lord Ganesha. You forbade me to utter his name."

The male frog said, "I am not that powerful. I have realised my mistake. Let us utter prayers in the name of Lord Ganesha."

Both of them started muttering Lord Ganesha's name. Incidentally, pitcher broke up to pieces. The danger to their life was gone. They jumped aside and said, "O Lord Ganesha, take away the misfortunes of all the creatures like us."

7

LITTLE GIRL AND GANESHA

(The story seems to reveal that unshakable faith pays, though one has to face problems at early stage. A common man does not think beyond worldly needs.)

Once Vinayaka Chaturthi mela was to be held in a nearby town. Many people from adjoining areas were preparing to visit it. A little girl from a poor family was very desirous of visiting the Mela. She requested her mother to permit her for it. Her mother said, “You are a little girl. The melas are generally crowded. You may be hurt there”. The little girl resisted again and again.

The mother said, “If you are too much interested in visiting Vinayaka Mela you do one thing for me. Take two laddoos and a pot of water with you. Give one laddoo to Vinayaka and offer water from this pot. You take second laddoo yourself.” The girl felt happy and took her mother’s offering with her.

She searched for Vinayaka in every nook and corner of the Mela but could not trace him. She was hungry. How could she take second laddoo before offering one to Vinayaka. She was a very obedient girl.

As the sun was about to set, Mela crowd became thinner and thinner. One of her neighbours said, “Little girl, Mela is over. Sun is about to set. Darkness will shroud the area. Accompany me to home.”

The girl said, "I am to offer this laddoo and water to Vinayaka. I am searching him. I would return only after completing my assignment."

The Mela was over. Everyone departed from the scene. She was all alone shouting, "Vinayaka, Vinayaka. Come and accept laddoo. I am hungry. I shall take my laddoo only after offering it to you from my own hands." Her cries made her emotionally surcharged. She cried nothing but Vinayaka.

Vinayaka saw this scene. He was moved by her faith and devotion. He appeared before her in the guise of an old Brahman and said, "I am Vinayaka. Offer this laddoo and water to me with your own hands and eat your share because you are hungry since morning."

After eating the laddoo and washing hand with the water, Vinayaka said, "I am pleased with your faith and devotion. Ask for any boon."

The little girl said, "I do not know what to ask and how to ask."

Vinayaka said, "Ask whatsoever you like."

The girl paused for a moment in a contemplated mood and said,"

"I want food.
I want wealth.
I want Lakshmi.
I want nine storeyed palace -
Illuminated with eighty four lamps -
Elephants moving in a corner-
Hansa swimming in a pool -
Maid servants grinding the corn -
Golden garlands hanging upon a peg.
Beautiful husband on decorated bed room -
Son playing in the cradle -
A son in my sister-in-laws lap -
Jingling bells around the bulls neck ,
Vinayaka, I want only this much."

Vinayaka was surprised to hear the little girl's demand. He said, "O, you are so little and your demands are so high. But I grant all this for you."

The girl rode back upon a bullock cart and reached home. Her mother said, “Why are you so late? I had been waiting for you throughout night. Everyone returned home by sunset. “

The girl related the whole story—how she reached for Vinayaka, how he accepted laddoo and water from her own hands and how he blessed her with wealth and other wordly belongings. Her mother was happy with the girl.

(The story teller says let wealth and other belongings received by the little girl may be possessed by one and all. The story teller further says that whosoever tells, listens or nods during this story be blessed by Vinayaka.)

8

VINAYAKA BLESSES A BOY

Once a boy quarrelled with his family. He left his house in search of Ganesha. He decided not to return till he met Ganesha. He went on and on till he reached the deepest and thickest jungles. Ganesha noticed his movements. He thought that the boy had left his house for my sake. It is my duty to protect him otherwise wild animals like lion and leopard would tear him to pieces.

Ganesha disguised himself as an old Brahman and followed him. He approached him and said, "O pretty boy, where are you going? What are you searching for? Do not you fear from wild animals like lions and leopards?"

The boy said, "I am in search of Ganesha. I want to have his "darshana" (glimpse). It is his duty to protect me. Why should I fear for a noble cause. I am his devotee."

The old Brahman observed his firm belief and said, "O my dear boy, I am pleased with your conviction. I am Ganesha in guise of old Brahman. I have protected you throughout your sojourn. None can harm you. Ask for any boon. I shall grant the same. But ask the boon only once."

The boy was pleased. His joys knew no bounds. He said, "O Lord Vinayaka, what should I ask from you?"

Vinayaka said, "It is at your own sweet will". The boy said,

"I want an elephant
With open seat on its back
I want dal-rice
Along with wheat snack,

And ghee mixed sugar
To get solace
A rosy cheek wife
Serving in a palace."

Vinayaka said, "O, you are a very clever boy. I never hoped such demands from you. But I bless you with all these possessions."

The boy returned home. His mother was surprised to see enormous wealth possessed by her son. He related the whole story to his mother.

(The story teller says let such prosperity visit to each and every one. He further says that whosoever relates or hears this story be blessed by Vinayaka.)

9

CHAUTH KI KAHANI

(The present story seems to reveal that money earned by one's hard labour is real wealth. Ladies can motivate their husbands for it. Any donation pays its dividend. It never goes waste.)

Once there lived a rich merchant. He had a married daughter. Whenever she visited his parental home his father used to say, "My dear daughter, what do you eat these days?" The daughter always said, "I take stale food." The father always felt sorry and showed sympathy to his daughter.

Once his son-in-law visited his in-laws village. The merchant said, "My daughter always complains that you serve her stale food. Why so?"

The son-in-law said, "She is not correct. We always serve fresh food to her. If you have any doubt please visit our village and observe it with your own eyes." The father-in-law nodded.

Once he visited his daughter-in-law without any prior information. He saw that the daughter was eating fresh breakfast. His daughter did not notice him. When she had taken her break fast the father came to her and said, "What have you taken today in your breakfast." His daughter said, "I have taken stale food today also."

The father got angry and said, "I have noted you taking fresh food and you still blame your in-laws for serving stale food. This is not good on your part."

The daughter said, "You try to understand my symbolic meaning of 'stale food', Neither my husband, nor his father do any business. They harp upon the earnings of their forefathers. They do not add any fresh wealth to it."

It was a sarcasting statement for the husband. He immediately reacted and said to his wife, "I accept your words in good spirit. I shall go out for business and would not return for twelve years till I store enough wealth."

Her husband left home that very day. His wife felt loneliness. One day she visited her neighbour's house. They were busy in listening some story. Some of them were preparing laddoos for 'Prasad'. The lady said out of sheer curiosity, "What are you doing today? Is today some special day?"

One old lady said, "Yes, today is Chauth Mata's day. We are listening her story."

The young lady said, "To whom this day is dedicated? What are its benefits? Please tell me. I am feeling uneasy, I too want to utilize my time in some useful activity."

The old lady said, "This day is devoted to Ganesha. Every 4th day of each fortnight of all lunar months belongs to Ganesha. We call this day as 'Chauth Mata day'. Having fast on this day blesses one with health, wealth and progeny. Your husband will return safe. If you observe fast on this day".

The young lady felt happy. She decided to observe that fast without telling it to her mother-in-law. Her mother-in-law offered her food for four times. But on fast days she gave her first meal to an unmarried daughter of a Brahman, second meal to cow. She hid the third meal behind the wall of her home so that small insects may feed on it. She took fourth meal herself after seeing the moon rise to break her fast. She continued this practice for twelve years.

On the twelfth year night she remembered her husband from the core of her heart and addressed to 'Chauth Mata', "My dear mother, will my husband return tomorrow? I have observed fast in your name. If he does not turn up, who will pinch faith in you in Kaliyuga era. Please accept my prayers."

The Chauth Mata heard her prayers. She appeared before her husband in dream and said, " Twelve years are over, you have amassed enough money. Your wife will be happy with it. Now she will not name her food as 'stale'. She misses you very much. You wind up your business. Have a happy union with her tomorrow."

The young business man murmured, " How can I wind up my business over night. I have to collect the lended money and to repay to my customers. It is an impossible work for me."

The Chauth Mata said, "Get up early in the morning. An unseen power will settle your accounts. The 'givers' and 'takers' would visit you automatically."

As he was murmuring in his sleep he turned his side and heard a thudding sound. He suddenly got up and recollected his dream. It was already early morning. He took his bath and started turning his accounts balance-sheets. To his great surprise he settled all the accounts in no time.

The young businessman started his home-ward journey. On his way he saw an old cobra shivering with cold. It was about to jump in the fire. The young man hissed it. The cobra was enraged. It said, "Why did you hiss me. I was fed up with my old age. I have missed my chance. Now I shall bite you."

The youngman said, "Now I am on my homeward journey. You can bite me when I return."

The snake followed him stealthily. The young man noticed it. His wife greeted her husband warmly. He set his bed up stairs. Before going to bed he spread soft sand on the first stair. On the second stair he placed some milk. On third stair he placed tub full of water. On the next stair he arranged some flowers. No one knew the reason of that act.

As the night fell the snake sneaked in to bite the young man. On the first stair it enjoyed the fun of crawling. On next stair it sipped milk. It had a bath in the tub. It smelt the flowers on the next stair.

As it moved onward 'Chauth Mata' was guarding the couple herself. She brought out her sword and cut the snake into pieces. A part of the head fell down in a shoe. The snake said to himself, " I shall hid myself in his shoes and bite him whenever he comes to put it on."

There was a big hole of the ants behind the wall where the young lady used to hid her third share of meal. The ants smelt some injured creature. They moved towards the snake. The head of the snake was still bleeding. They sticked to it in large number and ate it up.

The staircase was stained with blood. The old lady thought that some one has killed his son. She began to weep. The boy sensed the situation and shouted from upstairs, "Dear mother, I am safe. My enemy has been killed by some one."

The old lady thanked her stars. As the sun arose every one was surprised to see the strange happening. A neighbour lady said, "You are a fortunate mother. You must have completed some auspicious deed". The old lady humbly said, "No, no, I have no such thing to my credit. Better ask my daughter-in-law."

The daughter-in-law said, " Yes, I observed 'Chauth Mata' fasts without telling my mother-in-law because that may annoy her. The Brahman's unmarried girl can stand testimony to it because I parted with my first share of food to her as a donation. The other hint can be traced behind the wall where I used to hid my third share of meals for the insects.

The villagers went to the hind wall and dug the soil. To their great surprise they found a golden treasure under it. Every one thought it was due to "Chauth Mata's" kind blessings.

(The story teller says that one who tells or listens or nods, during this story will be blessed by 'Chauth Mata')

10
BENEVOLENT GANESHA

(The present story is a good example to explain that an individual has his or her own needs. Secondly a subtle use of language pays with dividend.)

Once there lived an old blind lady. She had a son and a daughter-in-law. She was very poor. She used to worship Ganesha. Ganesha used to say, "O old lady, I am pleased with your worship. Please ask for any boon. I shall grant you whatever you need."

The old blind lady used to say, "O, Ganesha, I do not know what to ask for."

Once Ganesha insisted for asking any boon. The old lady said, "I shall consult my family. I shall let you know my desires within a couple of days."

The old lady said to his son, "Ganesha is pleased with my worship. He wants to grant some boon. Please tell me what should I ask for?"

Her son said, "Dear mother, ask him to give enough money so that we may live a better life."

The old lady thought it proper to consult her daughter-in-law also. She said to her daughter-in-law, "Ganesha is pleased with my worship. He wants to grant some boon. Please tell me what should I ask for?"

The young lady said to her mother-in-law, "Please ask him for a grandson."

The old lady was confused because her son needed money and her daughter-in-law desired a son. She thought it proper to consult her neighbour also.

She went to her neighbour and said, "My dear lady, Ganesha is pleased with my worship. He wants to grant me some boon. Please tell me what should I ask for? My son needs money and my daughter-in-law needs a son."

The neighbour lady said, "Why should you ask for money or son. You are still to live for some years. Ask for your eyes and good health so as to pass remaining years honourably."

The old lady did not agree with her neighbour's advice also. She wanted some more time for the final judgement. She said to herself, "Why to displease my son and daughter-in-law. After all I am to live with them. Who else would look after me in still older days. Moreover why should I deceive myself, I must ask some thing for myself also."

Next day Ganesha appeared before her and repeated his old words. The old blind lady was well prepared to ask for her long cherished dream. She said, "O benevolent Ganesha, please grant eye-sight and health to me so that I would see my grandson taking rich food in golden utensils. Please grant grand-grandsons to my son and a purse of rupees nine crore."

Ganesha said, "O blind old lady, you have turned out a big cheat. You have deceived me by using very ornamental language. You have asked every thing. What else remains for a worldly man. But let your all desires be fulfilled."

After granting these boons Ganesha disappeared. The light was restored in old lady's eyes. As Lord Ganesha blessed old blind lady let everyone, who tells or listens this story be blessed by him. Let we also be blessed by Ganesha.

11

Widow Gardener And Vinayaka

(Apart from religious belief this story seems to reveal that elders should be kind and considerate towards the widows. The mother-in-laws should have regards for their daughter-in-laws because in return they would serve them in the last days of their life. The story also reveals that it is the initiative power which can uplift the downtrodden. One should work hard to live an honourable life. The youngsters too should be very considerate towards elders and forget their shortcomings.)

Once there lived a gardener's family. The old woman and her son used to look after them. The old lady was blessed with a son and a grandson. Her daughter-in-law also helped her in day-to-day work.

One day the old lady's son died due to sudden illness. It was like a bolt from the blue. The old lady turned violent towards her daughter-in-law because she took her as an illfated lady. She meted out to her a bad treatment. One day she scolded her and turned her out for two days. She sat outside her house but her mother-in-law had no pity for her.

The young lady left the home along with her son. She went here and there but could not find any shelter. One day she sat under a shady tree. Its shade was very soothing. She noted a temple not far away from this tree. It was Vinayaka's temple.

The passerby worshippers noted that helpless lady along with her young son. She got enough alm to make her both ends meet. One day she addressed to herself, "I belong to a gardener's family. I can collect flowers from some nearby garden. The devotees will purchase them. I can earn enough money. I can give better education to my son. I can construct my own house also."

She was-amused with this idea. She started collecting flowers in the name of Vinayaka, the governing deity of that area. In no time she earned enough money. She erected a little hut beside the shady tree. She sent her son to a nearby town for schooling.

The king's daughter also used to study in that school. Both of them became good friends. The boy was very beautiful. The princess was attracted towards him. The boy visited the king's palace off and on with the princess.

As the time passed the princess said to her mother, "I like that boy who studies with me and often visits our palace. I have developed a love for him. I have decided to marry him."

The queen was shocked when she knew her daughter's resolve. She refused her and said, "Ours is a royal family. Ours is royal blood. The boy belongs to an ordinary gardener's family. His mother lives in a thatched hut. This is disgrace to our family."

The princess repeated her resolve and said, "Either I shall marry that boy of my liking or remain unmarried throughout my life."

Impressed by the girl's resolve the king married his daughter to the flower seller's son. The king donated some villages and constructed a palace for them. They lived a happy life. The old lady devoted more and more time in Vinayaka's service.

On the other hand the mother-in-law in the village became a beggar. She left her home and collected alm from nearly villages. Once she heard about Vinayaka's temple and reached that shady tree where her daughter-in-law had took shelter some years back. She noted a beautiful palace nearby. She went to that palace in search of some job. Some official of that palace offered her some job of cleaning the utensils. She accepted the offer and worked there for a couple of days.

Once her daughter-in-law visited the kitchen and saw the old lady. The old lady said, "Whose palace is this? It is so beautiful as if it has been constructed by deities. It seems that the owner of this house has been blessed by ruling deity of this area—Lord Vinayaka. My daughter-in-law used to worship this deity. She left me due to my ill treatment. Now I feel sorry for it. If she meets me I shall beg pardon from her for my ill behaviour."

The lady recognised her mother-in-law. She was sorry for her wretched condition. She felt pity on her repentance and said, "Dear ma, the palace belongs to your own grandson, I am your daughter-in-law whom you turned out from the house. Vinayaka has bestowed all this upon us. Let us thank him. He has changed our fortune. (The story teller says let former days may not visit anybody. Let good fortune return to those who relate, listen and even nod to this story.)

12
GANESHA CUTS JOKE

(This is a rare humourous story. The story seems to reveal a public insult to a lady who does not respect her mother-in-law. Open repentance by a pretender is also reflected in the present story.)

Once there was an old lady. She had a son and her daughter-in-law. The family was not well off. Her son decided to go out for pretty trade to earn money. At the time of departure he advised his wife to look after his mother and to give her proper food.

As her son left for business the daughter-in-law thought of a plan to tease her mother-in-law. She took best of food in breakfast and spared some crumbs for the old lady. The old lady tolerated that behaviour because she did not want to create a trouble for a public show.

One day the old lady dared and said to her daughter-in-law, "I get nothing to take in my breakfast. Sometime I get some crumbs of dried ups and stale chapaties. What is this all about?"

The young lady said, "Our home is infested with rats. They must have eaten up your breakfast. As the chapaties are smeared with ghee and sugar, the rats are attracted towards them by sweet smell. Be careful in future. I cannot cook double breakfast."

The old lady remained silent and waited for her son's return. Twelve months were over. Her son was to return next day.

Ganesha noted the young lady's behaviour. He thought that she is blaming rats just for nothing. The rats have to visit other homes to feed them. He said, "I will teach her a lesson for the misery she has brought for the old lady."

The young lady went to sleep and bolted the door from inside. She put off her saree and placed it over a peg. She thought of getting early in the morning to finish the household work and to give a warm welcome to her husband.

Ganesha hinted the rats to drag her saree into some big hole. When the lady was fast asleep, the rats' battalion did their job as assigned by Ganesha.

The young lady's husband returned home in the early hours of morning and knocked at the door. The lady felt happy. She looked towards the peg to wear the saree before opening the door. She was shocked to see that the saree was missing from the peg. She saw that the bolt from inside was safe. Who could play that mischief ?

Her husband knocked the door again and again. The lady did not open the door. The husband became suspicious. Can it be a case of adultery? He shouted again and again. People from the neighbouring houses assembled in no time. They also knocked the door again and again but there was no reply.

The husband broke open the door with full force. The lady was sitting on her cot. She was very hesitant because she was without a saree. He scolded her and said, "How a saree can be misplaced from inside a bolted room?"

The young lady introspected and said to herself, "I always ate up my mother-in-law's breakfast and pretended that the rats has eaten it up. There is every possibility that Ganesha has incited the rats to drag my saree in their holes."

She invoked Ganesha and said, "O Ganesha, I have realised my mistake and your might. If you return my saree I shall offer one and a quarter maund laddoo to you. My character is at stake. I realise my mistake."

The young lady noticed that a part of her saree was visible in the big hole of a rat. She requested her mother-in-law to drag out the saree from the hole. She put on the saree and admitted her guilt publicly. She developed a special regard for Ganesha. Richness returned to their home in no time and they lived a happy life.

(The story teller says let suffering faced by the old and young lady may not visit to any body. Let happiness visit to those who tell, listen and even nod at the time of this story.)

Part-C

Lunar Monthwise Stories

CHAITRA

13

GANESHA BLESSED KING MAKARDHWAJA

(Ganesha Chaturthi Fast is observed on the 4th day of the waning moon, in the month of Chaitra, the first month of the Indian Lunar Calendar, i.e., Vikrama Samvat. The "Vikata" epithet (dreadful or great) of Lord Ganesha is especially worshipped on this day. It is believed that a fast on this day removes present or probable hurdles and bestows progeny to the barren ladies. It restores lost property also. A special "Havan" (offering an oblation with fire) with "bijaura" lemon added with pure ghee, is also performed. It seems that apart from religious belief the aim of the present story is to show that one should not hurt the religious belief of others. The elders should be considerate to the younger generation otherwise family intrigues and squabbles can disturb peace.)

Once Parvati asked Ganesha to tell her the story relating to Ganesha-Chaturthi fast which is observed on the 4th day of the waning moon in the month of Chaitra.

Ganesha said that in Satyayuga (First period of four Hindu Ages—the Golden age) there lived a king named Makardhwaja. He was very fond of his subjects. The people of his age were liberal, handsome, intelligent and pious. Unfortunately the king had no issue.

With kind blessings of Rishi Yajnavalkya he had a son. The king handed over the reign of his kingdom in his Minister's hand and looked after his son day and night.

His minister, Dharampal, became very rich. He had five sons. He arranged their marriage with pomp and show. They too began to enjoy a luxurious life.

Dharampal's youngest daughter-in-law was very religious minded. On 4th day of the waning moon, in Chaitra month, she observed fast and worshipped Ganesha. Her mother-in-law noticed it and said, "Do you want to overpower my son by "Tantra-Mantra"—(enchantment). She forbade her again and again not to observe fast and worship Ganesha but the daughter-in-law was firm on her conviction.

The mother-in-law was enraged and said, "O wicked woman, if you do not obey my command, I shall set you right by a good beating. I do not like this wicked performance."

The daughter-in-law said politely, "I am performing Ganesha-Chaturthi fast and worship. What is wickedness in it? The fast bestows good fate."

The mother-in-law did not pay any heed to her. She said to her son, "My dear son, your wife has resorted to witchcraft. I advised her many a times but she is a very impertinent lady. Set her right by suitable beating. I do not know who Ganesha is and why a fast is observed in his name. We belong to a royal family. What sort of difficulties can be removed by Ganesha?"

The son gave his wife a beating but she still observed her fast. After worship she said, "O Ganesha, kindly inflict my father-in-law and mother-in-law temporarily to set their mind right. They will definitely develop faith in you."

Ganesha immediately played a trick. He abducted king's son in the twinkling of an eye and hid him in Dharampal's palace. He threw his clothes and ornaments in king's palace and disappeared from the scene.

The king called his son again and again but there was no reply. He went to his minister's palace and enquired about the whereabouts of the prince. He told him that his clothes were in his palace but there was no trace of the prince. He did not know who committed that heinous sin. The king was so much horrified that he began to weep bitterly.

The minister said, "O aggrieved king, I do no know about your playful son. There is no gang of child lifter or dacoits in our kingdom. I shall search him out in all gardens and villages."

The king addressed his bodyguards and courtiers and said, "Search out my son immediately or you will be punished."

They searched each and every nook and corner but of no use. They reported the matter back to the king. The king was further shocked. When the abductor and the son could not be traced, he called his minister and said, "O Dharampal, tell me about my son. O blackguard, either trace my son or I shall kill you along with all the members of your family."

The minister was stunned to hear the king's verdict. He bowed and said, "I have never heard about any child abductor gang or dacoits in your kingdom, still I shall leave no stone unturned in search of your son."

Dharampal went to his palace to share his grief and sorrow with his family. He said, "If any one of you have any information about the prince's abductment tell me immediately. If the prince is not traced the king would crush the family to death."

The youngest daughter-in-law said, "O respected father-in-law, it is not a matter to worry about. Ganesha has inflicted us. Please worship Ganesha. If one and all from our kingdom observe his fast, the prince will return safe and sound. My words never fall short of my belief."

The father-in-law gained some confidence and consolation. He said, "O dear daughter-in-law, I have all praise for your pious belief. You will redeem my family tree. Please tell us how to worship Ganesha. I am a most unintelligent fellow. I do not know the greatness of this fast. O well fated lady, forgive us if we have committed any offence against you. Please tell us where is the prince?"

All the people of Makardhwaj's kingdom observed fast along with the king. Lord Ganesha was pleased with their devotion. He freed the prince. People were happy to see the prince in the palace. The king's joy knew no bounds. All of them said, "We have all praise for Ganesha. We too have all praise for minister's youngest able daughter-in-law. It is due to her guidance that my son has returned safe from the jaws of death. Let this fast be observed by all who wish safety of their progeny.

As Ganesha related this story to Parvati so did Krishna to Yudhishthira. Yudhishthira observed this fast and regained his lost glory and kingdom.

14

DHARMAKETU BRAHMAN AND LORD GANESHA

(Vakratunda, the curved trunk elephant, an epithet of Ganesha, is worshipped on the 4th day of waning moon in Vaishakha, the second month of the lunar calendar. It is believed that Ganesha protects the orphans. He washes away jealousy even from the enemy's mind and protects from all bad spirits. Apart from religious belief the story reveals that even one way good behaviour of a person can amend the behaviour of the rival.)

Once king Ranti Deva ruled over his kingdom. He conquered his enemies and befriended gods Yama, Kuber and Indra. A pious Brahman, Dharmaketu, also lived in his kingdom. He had two wives—Sushila and Chanchala. Sushila, as appears from her name, used to keep fasts. She became fragile, Chanchala never kept any fast and took full meal everyday.

In course of time Sushila gave birth to a female baby and Chanchala delivered a male baby. Chanchala used to pass remarks for Sushila because her pious life did not bear good fruit. Sushila was fed up with her husband's co-wife but she continued Ganesha Chaturthi fast.

Once Ganesha appeared before her and said, "O Sushila, jewels and pearls will come out from your daughter's mouth. You will be blessed by a son also. He will be a great scholar. follow your path without fear."

Due to Ganesha's blessings Sushila gave birth to a son and her daughter vomitted jewels and pearls. Unfortunately, Dharmaketu passed away and both the wives spent a life of widowhood.

Chanchala took into her possession all the belongings and lived in a separate house. Sushila lived in her old shattered home. But as her daughter vomitted jewels and pearls every day she recovered her richness and lived a better life. Chanchala became still more jealous of her.

Once Chanchala pushed her daughter into the well. Lord Ganesha protected her and she returned safe to her home. The girl related the whole story to her mother.

Chanchala was shocked to see the daughter alive. She begged pardon from Sushila with folded hands. She said, "O dear Sushila, you are very kind. I am very impious because I always pinpricked gentle and saintly people. I got nothing but illname and defame. I always remained with a disturbed mind. Please allow me to follow your path."

It is said that by the kind virtue and blessings of Lord Ganesha both the co-wives lived a happy life. It is believed that even the enemies become friends if Lord Ganesha is pleased. Lord Ganesha is the real cause of the change of heart of evil and wicked people.

15
DAYADEVA AND LORD GANESHA

(Aakhu Rath, an epithet of Ganesha (whose vehicle is rat), is adorned on the 4th day of the waning moon in the month of Jyeshtha, the third month of lunar calendar. People observe fast on this day to fulfil their desires. Ladies observe it to enjoy happy union with their husbands. Deserted wives believe that this fast will help them in regaining their husbands. Apart from religious belief the story reveals that one should remember gods even during good days also.)

King Prithu rules over this earth during Satyuga. A Dayadeva Brahman also lived at that time. He had four sons. He arranged marriages of all the sons according to rituals as written in Parashar Grihsutra.

Once his eldest daughter-in-law said to her mother-in-law, " Dear 'Sasuji', I have been keeping Lord Ganesha's fast right from my childhood. Kindly allow me to arrange all the rituals of Ganesha Chatruthi in this home also."

Her father-in-law said, "O dear daughter-in-law, you are eldest among all the fours. You are under no strain or trouble. You are not a mendicant. Why should you undergo such fasts? You enjoy your married life. Who is this Ganesha? How is he related to you?"

As time passed on, the eldest daughter-in-law became pregnant. She continued her fast. Her mother-in-law did not like it. She said, "Fasts will still tell upon your health. You will deliver a weak baby. I order you not to keep fasts."

The daughter-in-law left Ganesha-Chaturthi fasts to avoid family tussles. She gave birth to a son and in due course he attained adulthood. His grant father arranged his marriage.

When the boy was sitting under the marriage pandal for performing marriage ceremony, he was abducted by Ganesha in a mysterious way. Everybody was stunned to see his disappearance. The bride and her father were the most sufferers.

The eldest daughter-in-law said to her mother-in-law, " you insisted upon me to discontinue Ganesha Chaturthi fasts. We have annoyed Lord Ganesha. He must have abducted our son to punish us on this occasion."

The father-in-law and the mother-in-law felt sorry for their act but they were helpless. The would-be-bride and her mother-in-law decided to take Ganesha Chaturthi fasts till the bridegroom returns.

Once a hungry seer visited the bride's house and asked food. The lady arranged delicious food for the seer. The visiting seer was pleased by her hospitality. He said, "O dear daughter, ask for any boon and I shall bestow upon you the same. I am Ganesha myself. I have visited your house because you have pleased me by your unshakable faith and devotion''

The devoted lady said, "If you are pleased, please return me my husband." The seer said, "Your wishes will be fulfilled at the earliest."

Incidentally the abducted boy accompanied by some seer reached that township. Grandfather and the grandma were overwhelmed with joy. Tears rolled into their eyes. They embraced their grandson. They thanked Lord Ganesha because they got their grandson again.

The marriage pandal was re-erected. The left-up wedding ceremony was rearranged and performed as per rituals. The residents of that town and newly-wed bride thanked their stars. They still celebrate Ganesha Chaturthi as a remembrance of that holy day.

ASHADHA

16
King Mahijit Blessed By Lord Ganesha

(Lambodar or pot-bellied, an epithet of Lord Ganesha, is worshipped on the 4th day of the waning moon in the month of Ashadha, fourth month of lunar calendar. It is believed that Lambodar fulfils all wordly desires, blesses issueless couples with children and suppresses even dreaded enemies. Apart from religious faith the story tells that as a good ruler thinks for the betterment of his subject's so the subjects, also pray for his happiness otherwise they can invite some invader to get rid of him.)

King Mahijit ruled over Mahismati kingdom in Dwapara Yuga. He was extremely charitable, pious and glorious. He brought up his subjects like his children. But he had no son. All the worldly charms had no meanings for him because he knew that an issueless person cannot offer water to the deceased ancestors. He performed many "Yajnas" but all in vain. His youthhood was waning and old age was overpowering him day-by-day.

Once he called an assembly of knowledgeable people and said, "So far I know I have not committed any sin of any form in my life time. I never stockpiled wealth by torturing my subjects. I always ruled over this earth by following religious path. I punished the dacoits and bad characters, I arranged feasts for good friends. I always protected the Brahmans and cows and revered cultured persons. Still I have no son. Please ponder over this problem."

The esteemed gathering assured the king to find out some way at the earliest. A gathering of seers went to jungle to find out some Rishi-Muni who could bless the king or suggest some suitable way out of King's progeny.

Incidentally they spotted a Muni who was undergoing hard penance. People from nearby area told them that he had conquered anger. He had full knowledge of the real spirit. His name is Lomas because at the end of each "Kalpa" only one hair or "Rom" falls from his body.

After extending due courtesy one of the seers said, "We are here to remove our doubts. Please guide and help us."

Muni Lomus said, "Tell me your doubts and grief. Do not hesitate. Muni's penance is for removing citizens doubts and grievances."

One of the citizens from that group said, "We are from Mahismati Kingdom. King Mahijit rules that territory. He possesses all the qualities of a good king. He is very soft spoken. Parents give birth to children. It is the king who protects the citizens. Unfortunately our king has no son. Please tell us any fast, donation, worship or other religious ceremony which may help the king in having a son."

The Muni gave them a peaceful hearing and said, "I will tell you the secret of a fast which bestows children to the issueless persons and wealth to the poor. "Ganesha Chaturthi" fast will help your king in getting a son.

The Mahismati's citizens thanked Lomas Muni and returned back. They requested the king to keep Ganesha-Chaturthi fast. The king was pleased to hear the words from Lomas Muni. He observed that fast with full faith. As a result the queen Sudakshina became pregnant and after due time gave birth to a beautiful son. The king celebrated his sons's birth to satisfy the citizens. He gave alms to the poor and Dakshina or donation to the Brahmans for arranging and performing the rituals of the fast.

SHRAVANA

17
PARVATI WEDS SHIVA

(Ganesha Chaturthi fast is also observed on the 4th day of the waning moon in the month of Shravan, 5th month of Indian Lunar Calendar. It is believed that it gives happy married life to women and blesses them with son. Students get better education, poor get wealth, deported and tortured people return home with honour and people suffering from chronic health problems restore good health. This fast is a panacea for all worldly ills. Apart from religious rituals the story reveals that teacher's age or relation should not come in receiving knowledge. Ganesha, though Parvati's son, quenched the thirst of knowledge. Mother and son have no hesitation in exchanging knowledge.)

During satyuga, king Himalaya's beautiful daughter, Parvati, went to deeper forests for penance to get Shiva again as her life partner. But Shiva was not pleased with penance and did not appear before her. She recalled to her mind Ganesha and he presented himself immediately before her. Parvati said, "I have undergone a very dreaded penance to regain Shiva. Once you told me that you have heard from Narada about a fast related to you. Please tell me all the rituals of that fast so that I may fulfil my desire."

Ganesha said that the devotee should vow not to take food on the 4th day of the waning fortnight before moonrise. He or she should worship Ganesha before breaking fast. The devotee should take bath in white sesamum or "til" mixed in water. After routine prayer he or she should worship Ganesha. Ganesha idol can be of gold, silver, metallic or earthen according to one's capacity. Likewise the worshipping water pot or "Kalasha" should be placed at proper place. The idol may be worshipped with sixteen methods of worship or "Shodashopchar." The devotee should concentrate on Ganesha's different names like—Lambodar etc. The devotee should bow

before the idol and beg pardon for sins or other lapses. The idols may be offered various "prasad" dishes according to one's capacity. Laddoos are very much liked by Ganesha. Five laddoos may be given to the Brahman who may help in worship and the devotee may break his fast by eating five laddoos also.

The devotee should offer adorning water to the moon, uttering such words—O moon, you are born out of the milky ocean, you are goddess Lakshmi's brother. O moon, the maker of night, you accept my adoring water along with your wife Rohini. The devotee should bow before Ganesha and implore for fulfilling the desires. The devotee should offer food to the Brahman and to his family members. The Ganesha's idol may be given to one's Guru along with suitable offerings. Lord Ganesha may be given honourable farewell.

One can continue Chaturthi fast life long, or for 21 years, for one year or only once in a year as one can afford. The "Uddyapan" or accomplishing ceremony of this fast may be completed on the 4th day of the waning moon in the month of Shravana.

It is believed that Parvati observed this fast with full faith and Lord Shiva was pleased with her devotion. At last she got Shiva and married him.

It is said that this story was related to Parvati by Swami Kartikeya. This very story was related by Lord Krishna to Yudhishthara when he was in jungles during exile period. Yudhishthara observed Ganesha Chaturthi fast and attained his kingdom back from the Kauravas.

BHADRAPADA (SHUKLA PAKSHA – I)

18

GANESHA CURSED MOON GOD

(Main Ganesha Chaturthi is celebrated on the 4th day of the bright fortnight in the month of Bhadrapada. Seeing moon on this day is prohibited. It is believed that it brings false blemish to the onlooker. On this day Ganesh Puja is performed in day time. In local dialect this day is known as "Danda Chauth" because the onlooker of the moon is punished by this or that false pretext.

Every Lunar "tithi" or lunar date has one controlling god or goddess. The controlling authority of "Chaturthi" is Ganesha. It was on this day that Moon, due to its beauty, made sarcasting remarks on Ganesha for his ugly looks.

Apart from religious belief, this story reveals that everything made by nature has its own beauty. It should not be looked down by any one. Once Moon looked down upon Ganesha. So people shun him on this day and do not like to have its glimpse. The story also reveals that even jokes take serious turns. When Krishna saw Syamantaka Mani with Satrajita he said, "I like this Mani very much. I deserve to possess it."

That was 4th day of Bhadrapada in bright half fortnight. Even one remark cost Krishna a lot and aroused family discord).

Krishna was falsely blemished for grabbing Syamantaka Mani by most of the people just for nothing. Krishna was fed up with these accusations. He requested Narada to tell him the cause of such a public feeling about him.

Narada told Krishna that he had a glimpse of the moon, on the 4th day of the bright fortnight in the month of Bhadrapada. If someone sees moon on that day he earns false accusation.

Krishna said to Narada, "Respected Rishi, the moon is so beautiful. It attracts even small children. Its rays shower nectar on earth. On second day "in the bright fortnight people wait

for its appearance in the sky to have its glimpse. The moon's glimpse blesses the on-lookers. Why the moon's glimpse is forbidden. Please clear the mystery behind it."

Narada said that in olden days Brahma, Vishnu and Mahesha offered Ashtasiddhi and Navanidhi to Ganesha as his wives. Later on he was declared as a "first worshipped" god among gods. All the three sang songs in his praise.

Ganesha was highly pleased and said to Brahma, "I am happy with your selfless devotion and praise. You ask for any boon. I shall fulfil it."

Brahma said, "O first laudible God, I want to create new universe. I wish that there should be no hindrance in my work."

Ganesha smiled and said, "Let it be so."

After getting the desired boon Brahma returned to his "Loka". On the other hand Ganesha leaving behind "Satyaloka" turned towards "Chandraloka." Ganesha was in his extra-ordinary strange form. The beautiful moon (Chandrama) gazed at the disproportionate parts of Ganesha which were laugh provoking, Ganesha bore long trunk, winnowing basket like ears, extended heavy belly. He was riding on a mouse. Seeing such a look the beautiful Chandrama could not help laughing.

Ganesha became angry on "Chandrama" (moon). His eyes became blood red. He said, "Chandrama" (moon), you are so charming and beautiful. Why do you laugh at me? You seem to be proud of your beauty. You would have to suffer for this mockery. From this day onwards, no one would look at your sinful face. If some one looks at you, even by mistake, he has to bear false blemish."

Narada said to Krishna that on hearing this curse the entire world fell into deep lamentation. Chandrama's face faded. Out of shame he hid himself in the ocean for a long time.

All Gods, Rishis and Gandharvas were disappointed on Chandrama's disappearance. All of them went to Brahma under Indra's leadership. After paying regards they related the story of Chandrama's disappearance and curse upon him by Ganesha.

Brahma contemplated for a while and said, "No one can reverse Ganesha's word. All the three gods—Brahma, Vishnu and Mahesha are helpless before him. This is no exaggeration. Take his refuge. Only he and he alone can free 'Chandrama' from that curse."

The gods implored, "O Brahma, how can we please him? Kindly tell us the proper way out."

Brahma told them to worship Ganesha on the 4th day of the black half fortnight of the month to offer proper articles like laddoos and to keep fast in his name.

The gods asked "Vrihaspati" (Jupitor, Juno), the preceptor of gods, to visit Chandrama and to explain him the way-out as suggested by Brahma. Vrihaspati went to Chandrama and appraised him about the ways and means to please Ganesha.

Chandrama worshipped Ganesha by performing proper rites as told by Brahma. Ganesha was pleased and appeared in playful mood.

Chandrama praised Ganesha and said, "O Omnipresent, O all prevading, you are the basic cause of all causes.O Omniscient, you are a worth knowing secret, Please smile at me, please bless me. I have realised your might. Those who think otherwise about you, cannot get a space even in the hell."

Hearing such praise-worthy words from Chandrama's mouth Ganesha smiled in a loud roaring voice like a thundering cloud. He said, "I am highly pleased with you for your realisation and repentance. You ask for any boon. I am willingly prepared to grant you the same."

Chandrama said, "O God, let all people have my glimpse as before, with due regard. Let my sin and curse disappear with your kind blessings."

Ganesha said, "O Chandrama, I would bless you with some other boon. I shall not withdraw my previous words."

All the gods trembled when they heard Ganesha's verdict. They implored with one voice, "O Ganesha, you are kind to your devotees. Please free Chandrama from his curse. We beg this boon from you. Please have regard to old Brahma."

Ganesha was moved by their sincere appeal. He said, "Those who will see Chandrama on the 4th day of the bright fortnight of this month will definitely earn false blemish. There is no doubt in it. But those who will see Chandrama on 2nd day of each month in the bright fortnight, will not be blemished even if they see Chandrama on the 4th day of the increasing moon in Bhadrapada."

Narada told Krishna, in this way why people wait for having a glimpse of Chandrama on second day of the bright fortnight every month.

Ganesha again said, "Those who would observe fasts on the 4th day of the waning moon in every month and worship you along with your wife, Rohini, would never be blemished."

Narada said, "O Krishna, you also observe these fasts. you will never be blemished in future."

BHADRAPADA (SHUKLA PAKSHA – II)

19

SYAMANTAK MANI – I

(Maha Ganesha Chaturthi or Ganesha Chaturthi festival is celebrated on the 4th day of the bright fortnight in the month of Bhadrapada, the sixth month of the Indian Lunar Calendar. It is believed that Ganesha was born on this day at midnoon. In this month this fast is observed in bright and dark fortnight i.e., in Shuklapaksha and Krishnapaksha.)

It is believed that whosoever observes this fast is emancipated from blemish or false accusation. A devotee wins his law suit. This fast washes away all sort of worldly worries. It helps in earning wealth, fame and knowledge. It curbs enmity among brothers, husbands and wives. It also helps in regaining lost power or property. Ladies can please their father-in-law, mother-in-law and mothers by keeping this fast.

The devotee should get up early in the morning and must take bath with white 'til' or sesamum. As Chandradarshan (Looking the moon) is forbidden, so worshipping ceremony may be completed by mid-noon.

This day is specially celebrated in Rajasthan and Maharashtra in a big way.

It seems that this story tells that gods can be pleased by hard devotion. Excessive wealth puts one into great trouble.

Even gods and greatmen are not beyond suspicion if they are entrapped in its lust. It can bring big stigma on them. A suspicion is difficult to be removed but one should try one's best to be above board.

In good olden days Saunakadi Rishis were sitting in Naimisharanya "Tirtha" (a place of pilgrimage). They requested Vyas to show them the path to accomplish every work without any impediment. Which god they should worship to accomplish their goals?

Vyas said, "This very question was asked by Yudhishthira from Krishna when they were planning to attack Kauravas. Krishna told them to worship Ganesha who is born out of Parvati's filth. Krishna also told them as how and when to worship Ganesha. By worshipping Ganesha they should take as if they have worshipped Vishnu, Shiva, Sun, Parvatī etc. This "Puja" was once performed in Shivaloka.

Sanatkumar said, "O Vyas, who observed this fast for the first time and why?"

Vyas said, "I shall relate an interesting story in this regard."

The learned gathering nodded and he continued with the story. He said, "This fast was first observed by Vasudeva Jagannath Krishna to free him from a false blemish."

Sanatkumar said, with great surprise, "Generally Krishna is known as the Creator, Supporter and Destructor of the Universe. He is considered as a great soul among all souls. How he earned a blemish? Who casted aspersion on him?"

Vyas told the sacred gathering, "Narada Muni advised Krishna to observe this fast. I shall tell you the real story. Long long ago, Krishna and Balrama incarnated on this earth to free it from sins. Jarasandha, the ruler of Magadha, invaded Yadava's territory time and again. He looted their territory and insulted their women folk. Krishna was fed up with day-to-day attacks. He asked Vishvakarma to build a golden capital, Dwarka, in the mid of ocean. All the queens had separate palaces. All the worldly pleasures were available to the residents of that city.

There lived a Yadava lord, named Ugra. He had two sons—Satrajit and Prasenjit. Satrajit underwent a great penance to please Sun god. The Sun god was pleased and appeared before him. Satrajit was delighted to see Sun god. Satrajit uttered praiseworthy words for Son god such as—"You are self illuminated, you are son of Kashyapa, you illuminate moon, I bow before you time and again."

The Sun god said, "I am highly pleased with you. Ask for any boon. If you do not ask for any, I present you Syamant Mani (diamond) which I always wear around my neck. It will give you "Ashtabhar" gold daily (nearly 24 maunds). But be chaste before wearing it. If the bearer is unchaste it can bring death."

The Sun god disappeared and Satrajit adored the Mani around his neck. When he was returning to Dwarka, he was dazzling like a Sun. People recognized him only when he came very nearer to them. Krishna was coveted to see the Mani but he never tried to possess it. From Krishna's facial expression Satrajit guessed that he wanted to possess it or he may demand it from him. So he handed it over to his brother Prasenjit with instruction that he would wear it only if he is in chaste position.

Once Prasenjit went for hunting with Krishna. He was wearing the Mani in unchaste condition. A lion killed Prasenjit. Jambawan killed that lion and took the Mani with him, and gave it to his son. On the other hand Krishna returned to Dwarka along with other fellow hunters.

When people saw Krishna without Prasenjit they apprehended that "he must have been killed by Krishna because he wanted to possess the Mani. A greedy person can commit any sin. Such a person can kill even his guru."

Krishna was distressed by false blemish. He did not utter any word and left Dwarka along with few friends to the place where Prasenjit was killed by the lion. He followed the foot-prints of the lion which ended near a cave.

Krishna entered into the cave. It was dark and dingy. People waited outside the gate. He went deeper and deeper and to his great surprise saw a palace where a boy was playing with Syamantak Mani and a beautiful girl was rocking the cradle. She was singing a lullaby—A lion killed Prasenjit, your father killed that lion. Do not weep O little Prince, Syamantak diamond is thine.

The lady smiled and felt lovesick to see Krishna. She advised him to leave the cave otherwise her father would not spare him. Krishna was not a coward. He blew his Panchjanya conch to challenge Jambawan. Jambawan could not tolerate it and appeared on the scene. Both the warriors were interlocked in fierce duel battle for 21 days. Krishna crushed Jambawan's ego. Jambawan recollected his previous life and said, "O Krishna, you were Rama and conquered Ravana. Please pardon me for my foolish behaviour."

Krishna blessed him by putting his hand on Jambawan's head. He said, "I have been accused due to this Syamantak Mani. It is rumoured in Dwarka that I have killed Prasenjit and stolen it. Please hand it over to me to free me from false blemish."

Jambawan read some message in his daughter Jambawati's eyes and said to Krishna, "O Krishna, I offer my daughter's hand to you as your wife. I also present Syamantak Mani to you as dowry. Please take both with you with great honour."

On the other hand Krishna's fellowmen, who were waiting outside the cave returned to Dwarka after seven days and declared Krishna dead in that cave. The citizens were shocked and performed his last rites.

When Krishna returned to Dwarka along with Jambawati and Syamantak Mani, people's joy knew no bounds. They celebrated his return. Krishna related them the whole story of his combat with Jambawan and they freed him from false blemish. Krishna returned Syamantak Mani to Satrajit in the presence of all the courtiers.

Satrajit felt ashamed and he offered Satyabhama—his daughter to Krishna as his wife.

BHADRAPADA (SHUKLA PAKSHA – III)

20

SYAMANTAK MANI – II

Once Krishna recovered Syamantak Mani from Jambawan and returned it to Satrajit. Two Yadavas—Satvadhanwa and Akrur—became jealous of Satrajit.

Once Krishna was away from Dwarka. Satvadhanwa killed Satrajit and took Syamantik Mani in his possession.

When Krishna came back, Satyabhama related the whole story of Satrajit's death. But it was again rumoured that Krishna was ill-hearted. Either he wants to possess Syamantaka Mani again or he has already grabbed it.

Krishna sensed the matter. He said to Balrama, "Respected brother, Satvadhanwa has killed Satrajit for the sake of Mani and now he is about to flee from Dwarka with his possession. We deserve that Mani by all means. The Mani is ours."

Satvadhanwa came to know that Krishna and Balrama were conspiring to repossess Syamantak Mani. He was horrified to see the writing of his death on the wall. He stealthily handed over it to Akrur. Satvadhanwa wanted to hid himself to far off place. He ascended a mare and set for a long travel in Southern lands. Krishna and Balrama sat on a chariot and followed him. They followed him for 400 miles. His mare fell dead. He ran on foot. They still followed him. At last Krishna killed him then and there. Balrama was still sitting on the chariot.

Krishna shouted from below and said, "My dear brother, I could not recover Syamantak Mani from him. I am so sad and sorry for it."

Balrama could not believe his words. He said, "Krishna, you always manoeuvre things. I have never seen any greedy and sinner person like you. When you do not miss to kill your nearer and dearer for the sake of wealth who would stand by you?"

It was again a strange experience for Krishna because he was falsely blemished by his own elder brother. Krishna tried to please Balrama by taking a solemn oath.

Balrama was not convinced with Krishna's solemn oath. He said, " I do not believe in a cavil ("Mithyawad"), I cannot tolerate this nuisance any more. I say good-bye to you."

Balrama left for Barar (Vidarbha) country-side. Krishna rode on his chariot and returned to Dwarkapuri. People came to know that Krishna had returned alone. He has annoyed Balrama. They rumoured that Krishna had not acted well by expelling Balrama from Dwarka. It did not become him to behave in such a way for the sake of Syamantak Mani.

Krishna could not bear this public slander. He felt rejected and dejected.

On Krishna's return Akrur felt uneasy. He was having a sense of guilt due to Satvadhanwa's innocent killing. He fled from Dwarka under the pretext of some long pilgrimage. He settled in Kashipuri and arranged various types of "Yajna" to please gods. He produced maunds of gold everyday by the magic Syamantak Mani and distributed among people to please them. He won over many religious scholors by building many temples in the name of various gods and goddesses. He wore that Surya Mani in full chaste condition. As a result there was no famine or any mental or physical type of agony to the people wherever he went.

Krishna was omniscient and so knew every thing about Akrur. As he was an incarnate in form of a man he always played ignorance as a trick.

As Krishna was falsely blemished time and again and he had to face anguish of Balrama, his elder brother, he thought it proper to consult some seer for these accusations. Once Krishna was in palsy mood when Narada Muni appeared before him. Krishna paid him due courtesy and offered him "aasan" to sit on.

Narada read Krishna's mood and said, "Why do you look so sad? What sort of worry pinches you? O Krishna, reveal the whole story before me. Perhaps I could help you."

Krishna politely said, "O Deva Rishi Narada, I am being falsely blemished time and again. I am so sorry for it. I want to take refuge under your kind shadow. Please free me from my worry."

Narada said, "Dear Krishna, I know the real cause of false accusation. Incidentally you had a glimpse of the moon on the 4th day of the bright fortnight in the month of Bhadrapada. Seeing moon on that night is inauspicious.

"The Mani is with Akrur. He must be called before the courtiers. Let him show that Mani publicly so that people may not accuse you."

Krishna send messengers to Akrur. Akrur appeared before the courtiers and showed the Mani publicly. In this way Krishna became free from false blemish.

BHADRAPADA (KRISHNA PAKSHA)

21

Nala-Damyanti Reunited

(Ganesha Chaturthi fast is also observed on the 4th day of the waning moon, in the month of Bhadrapada, the 6th month of Indian Lunar Calendar. It is believed that Lord "Ekdanta" or One tusked epithet of Ganesha, blesses the king or a person whose kingdom or property has been usurped by some one, if he or she observes fast on this day. The story of Nala-Damyanti, a legendary couple, is also associated with this fast.

Apart from a legendary story the theme reveals that gambling invites unrelatable difficulties in the family. A distressed man can abondon his wife. A woman can face tremendous difficulties and still she remains a devoted wife.)

Once Raja Veersain ruled over Nishadha. His son, Nala was very handsome. He was very fond of horses. He was a good horse-rider also. He was married to Damyanti, the beautiful princess of the king of Vidarbha. She gave birth to a son and a daughter, named Indersen and Indersena.

Once Kali, the ruler of 4th age (iron age), was annoyed with Nala. He wanted to persecute Nala. He waited for twelve long years but got no chance. Once he thought of a plan. He entered into the body of Nala and incited him for gambling.

Pushkar, Nala's brother, was expert in dice-game. Once Nala and Pushkar were engaged in a dice-game. Kali guided

Pushkar in dice throwing. He misguided Nala in every dice-throw. Nala lost his kingdom and became very poor. Pushkar became the ruler of Nishadha kingdom.

Nala left Nishadha along with his wife, Damyanti and his children. Once he was resting under a tree. A strange bird flew away with Nala's only cloth. Nala felt ashamed. He removed Damyanti's piece of cloth when she was in deep slumber and disappeared in dire disappointed state of mind.

When Damyanti got up from her sleep, she was shocked to note that Nala was not there and her cloth was missing. She was in great despair and in a disappointment state. She lamented and wailed time and again, She decided to go back to her parental home, Vidarbha but she lost her way. Her children were also separated from her.

Nala also suffered a lot. He went to Ayodhya in search of some job. He disclosed his name as Bahuk before the king Rituparna. He offered him a job of a charioteer as he had been a good horse rider.

Damyanti, while loitering in state of a beggar met Maharishi Sharbhanga. She bowed before him. She said, "O Rishi Sharbhanga, when will I be reunited with my lost husband? How could I restore my lost status when our palace had amply elephants and horses of best breeds? When my fortune would return? Please guide me and tell me some ways and means to fulfil my desire."

Maharishi Sarbhanga said, "O aggrieved Damyanti, do not feel desperate. I will show you a right path. You observe fast of "Ekdanta" Ganesha in the month of Bhadrapada on 4th day of the waning moon."

Damyanti returned to her parental home and related her grief to her father. She observed this fast continuously on Ganesh Chaturthis. Ganesha was pleased with her faith and devotion.

Once a sadhu came and said to the king of Vidarbha, "O king, your daughter Damyanti is a beautiful lady. Why do not you arrange "Swayamvar" for your daughter's marriage? Give it a wide publicity. There is every possibility that Nala may also appear as a suiter. If he comes in disguise, your daughter will recognise him because she is too much in love with him. These days she is undertaking Ganesha's fast for attaining re-union."

King Vidarbha liked that idea and rearranged "Swayamvar" ceremony for his daughter. Even Lord Indra disguised himself as Nala and came as a suiter. For Nala also the news of Damyanti's Swayamvar was heartening. He became very clumsy due to Kali's punishment and hard work.

Nala joined the "Swayamvar" ceremony and stood in one corner of the suiters. Damyanti went around the arena. She halted before deceitful Nala-Indra. She noticed that his eye-lids were not falling and rising. She sensed the game. She again had a round and spotted Nala, who was in a shabby condition. She put the winner garland in his neck. All the suiters were shocked to see her choice. Indra, the deceitful Nala, disappeared from the scene. This was a second surprise for the suiters. It did not take much time for the gathering to know the reality. She was reunited with her husband after three years separation.

Kali forgave Nala. Raja Nala again had gambling with Pushkar and regained his kingdom. Damyanti thought that it was all due to Lord Ekdanta Ganesha's blessings. By regaining her husband, and children, she enjoyed a happy life for many years.

Lord Krishna related this story to Yudhishthira and assured him that by keeping this fast he would also regain his lost kingdom.

ASHVINA

22

SHRI KRISHNA AND BANASUR

(Ganesha Chaturthi fast is also observed on the 4th day of the waning moon, in the month of Ashvin, the 7th month of Indian Lunar Calendar. Krishna Ganesha or cloud like Ganesha, is worshipped at this occasion. It is believed that this fast annihilates all sorts of worldly adversities. It helps in conquering all enemies and restoring lost son and kingdom. The devotee should shun anger, pretension and greed. A "Havan" with "Haldi" (turmeric) and grass is considered very pious.

The story reveals the passion of sex and its influence. Even demons seek power from gods, though they use it for ill ends.)

Once Banasur's daughter, Usha, met prince Aniruddha, son of Pradumna, in her dream. She became so much passionate and sexually disturbed that she could not control herself. She asked her friend Chitralekha to draw sketches of all sort of creatures. When she saw Prince Aniruddha's sketch, she was overjoyed and said to Chitralekha, "I saw this man in my dreams. I want to marry him. Please search him out from any corner of the world. If you do not I shall sacrifice my life."

Chitralekha assured her to search out Aniruddha and to present him before her. She trodded the whole world and at last reached Dwarka. As she belonged to a Rakshasha family so she could enchant anybody. She went inside Aniruddha's palace. He was in deep sleep. She abducted him along with his coat. In the early hours of the morning she reached Banasur's capital.

The courtiers and the spies tried their best to search out prince Aniruddha but all in vain. It was a shocking jolt for king Pradumna because his son could not be traced. He sensed some foul play. The news was known to Krishna who was Pradumna's father and Aniruddha's grand father. He too, was disturbed. Rukmani, Anuraddha's grandma, was also shocked to know this news. She wailed and wept before Krishna and said, "Who has abducted our grand son? Has he disappeared at his own will? What happening forced him to leave his home? Either present him before my eyes or I shall end my life at my own will."

Seeing that scene Krishna was badly perturbed. He called his fellow brethren's conference to handle the situation. Lomas Rishi appeared on the scene and enquired about the problem.

Lord Krishna said, "O respected Rishi, my grand son has disappeared. I do not know whether some one has abducted him or he disappeared himself. His mother is under great stress. Please help us."

Rishi Lomas said, "I just met Narada Muni. He told me that Chitralekha, Usha's companion, has abducted him. At present he is safe and sound in Usha's palace. Banasur has blessed her daughter Usha to marry him. At present you observe Ganesha Chaturthi's fast. You will gain enough power to conquer him."

Krishna heeded to Rishi's advice and observed Sankat-Chaturthi's fast as per ceremony. Later on Krishna attacked Banasur. Even Lord Shiva helped Banasur but Krishna crushed Banasur's one thousand hands due to Ganesha's blessing. Krishna restored Aniruddha to Rukmani. Since that day people observe this fast to get back their lost relations. Those desirous of world tour or pilgrimage must observe this fast.

KARTIKA (KRISHNA PAKSHA – I)

23
DAITYARAJ VRITRASUR

(Lord Ganesha's Sankashta Chaturthi fast is also observed on the 4th day of the waning moon, in the month of Kartika, 8th month of Lunar Calendar. The "Ping" (reddish brown) epithet of Ganesha is especially adorned on this day. Horse bean, mixed with ghee is poured in the "Yajna". The devotee does not speak while taking meal. It is believed that the devotee fulfils his desires and conquers enemies through this fast. It is also said that if some one just listens this story, he is blessed for progeny and attains the benefits of Ashva Medha and "Vajapeya Yajna". Apart from religious belief, the present story reveals that evil forces try to overpower thinkers, philosophers and broad hearted people just for pleasure, but the latter should not lose heart. They must device some means to supress evil forces for ever for the larger interest.)

Once demon Vritrasur conquered the universe and enslaved all the deities. He expelled all the deities from their respective territories. As a result the deities ran helter-skelter in all the ten directions. At last they took refuge in Lord Indra's kingdom. They implored him for help in restoring their lost territory.

Lord Indra said, "The demons have made Ocean as their permanent abode. Taking it as a safe abode they have become fearless, impertinent and powerful. Moreover they have secured a boon from Brahma that they are invincible and could not be killed by any mightiest warrior. Better you go to Agastya Rishi. Please him by your devotion and prayers. He can suck the entire ocean as he is "pot born." If the ocean becomes empty and marshy, their power and strength will shrink to nothingness. Having been deprived from their power they will take shelter in their parental land and you will again gain heaven. Only he and he alone can come to your help."

Getting sincere advice from Lord Indra they went to Agastya Rishi's Ashrama. Agastya Rishi was under deep concentration and contemplation. They sang eulogy to please the Rishi. The Rishi opened his eyes and the deities paid "Ashtanga Pranam" by prostration of the eight parts of the body. The Rishi was pleased with their eulogy and low obeisance. He smiled and said, "What cause brings you here? Have you been tortured by demons? Have you been expelled from your respective seats of contemplation? Tell me frankly with each and every detail. I shall fulfil your desires."

The deities related their awful tale. Agastya Rishi said, "You return to your seats of contemplation. I shall find out some way to dry up the entire ocean."

The deities returned to their respective abodes. Agastya Rishi said to himself, "The ocean is spread over one lac "Yojana" (eight lac miles). How can I suck it inside my belly"?

The Rishi invoked Lord Ganesha. He also observed Ganesha Chaturthi fast on that day. He observed this fast for three successive months. Lord Ganesha was pleased with him. He blessed enough power to Rishi. With his kind blessing he sucked the whole ocean in no time. The Demon's island became guardless. Without ocean they lost their glory. The deities restored their seat of learning and contemplation. It is believed that since that day this fast is observed by the devotees.

According to a version this story was related to Parvati by Ganesha himself. Krishna related this story to Yudhishthira. Yudhishthira observed that fast and won back his kingdom.

KARTIKA (KRISHNA PAKSHA – II)

24

KARVA CHAUTH

(This story is related on the 4th day of the waning moon in the month of Kartika, the eighth month of Indian Lunar Calendar. Ladies relate this story in the afternoon. They offer "Karka" or "Karva" (earthen or sugarmade pot) to elderly ladies and touch their feet. The fast is broken after seeing the moon rise. The fast is observed by married ladies for the well being of their husbands. In certain families husbands also take this fast for the well-being of their wives. Apart from religious belief the story seems to preach that one should not interfere others, in completing a religious resolve. Ladies should have sympathetic attitude towards their fellow sex. Unshakeable faith pays in the long run. Early marriage can bring disaster to ladies because they cannot perform many religious ceremonies properly.)

Once a rich businessman had seven sons. He had only one daughter also. All the brothers and sister used to take their meal together.

Their only sister got married in early age. As a religious ceremony, their sister was to observe her first "Karva Chauth" fast after marriage. Their sister observed her fast for the first time. As the moon was to rise long after sunset on the 4th day of the waning moon, her brothers were worried about her delayed meal.

They thought a plan to make her see a false moon on the mountain. One of her brothers, climbed the peak of a mountain. He took a "Chalni" (sieve) and placed it on the mountain. He put a big lamp behind the "chalni". It looked as if moon was rising. The other brothers said, "Dear sister, look towards the mountain. See the moon rise and break your fast."

The young girl asked her seven sister-in-laws to see the moon and break their fast. They said, "It may be a moon for you. We will not believe it. You break your fast if you so like."

The girl, due to early marriage, was too young to understand her brother's and sister-in-law's message.

She sat to break her fast. As she took her first morsel she noted a hair in it. It was a bad omen. She took her second morsel. She noted some fungus in it. When she took her third morsel a messenger from her in-law's house knocked at the door and said, "Your sister's husband is seriously ill. Send her immediately with me."

Every body in the family was nonplussed. She tried to open her dressing box thrice but noted bad omens. She had to put on white dress. Her sister-in-law tied a Mohar (gold coin) in the corner of her saree. She was advised to bow and touch the feet of all women, whosoever meet her on the way. She was further advised to donate the gold coin to that lady who bless her for "suhag" (unwidowhood).

She came across many women. She bowed and touched their feet. All of them blessed for her brothers' and sister-in-law's prosperity. None of them blessed for her husband's health and long life.

When she reached her father-in-law's house her young sister-in-law (nand) was standing on the doorstep. This young lady touched the girl's feet. As a blessing she said, "Let your life be peaceful, let your seven brothers live a happy life along with their wives, let your breadearner (husband) live a long life."

The lady was pleased with the girl's blessings. She untied the knot of her saree and offered gold coin to her. She again tied the knot on the corner of her saree.

When she entered the house, her mother-in-law did not offer "peetha" (seat) to her. Instead she said, "Go to that side, you will get a "Mudha" (high seat)." She went upstairs. She was shocked to see her husband's dead body. She sat beside it and began to serve him by removing the flies with the help of the corner of her saree.

Her mother-in-law called the maidservant and said, "Take this stale food to that widow who is responsible for my son's death."

The young lady spent one month with the dead body. On the 4th day of "Mangsir" month the Chauth Mata entered that street and shouted in such taunting words,—"Purchase "Karva" (earthen pot), O lady who can see moon in day time, take karva from me. O killer of one's own husband take "karva" from me."

The unfortunate young lady came down and said, "O Mother Karva Chauth, you have marred my fate by forcing widowhood upon me. You are powerful enough to make my fortune again. For God's sake have pity on me. Return my husband's life. I am too young."

The Chauth Mata said, "Next month is 'Pausha.' Pausha Mata will visit your street. She is more powerful. She will return your husband's life." With these words Karva Chauth disappeared from the scene.

Next month, Pausha Mata assured her that "Magha Mata" will visit next month and give life to her husband. Likewise months after months "Chaitra Mata", "Baishakha Mata", "Jyeshtha Mata", "Ashadha Mata", "Shravana Mata", "Bhadrapada Mata" came one by one and assured her that the Mata of next month is powerful than the former. The young lady still preserved and protected her husband's body. She always felt that she had not committed any sin deliberately. Why should she be punished.

Next came Ashvina Mata. She said, "Kartika Mata" is annoyed with you. She will visit your street next month. She will return your husband's life. You catch hold her feet with full firmness." Ashvina Mata left her by giving sincere advice.

Next came Kartika Mata. She shouted in anger, "O beloved sister of seven brothers, purchase 'karva' from me. O killer of one's own husband, take 'karva' from me. O breaker of Karva Chauth fast, take 'karva' from me."

The young lady was well prepared for her visit. She bowed before her. She caught her feet with full firmness and began to weep. She said most humbly, "O Kartika Mata, my 'Suhag' has been looted at such an early age. No one has the least sympathy for a widow. My mother-in-law taunts me as killer of her son. For the last one year I have been hoping against hope for the return of my husband's life. All the Matas visiting earlier expressed their unwillingness for my husband's life saying that you are the most powerful among them. Please bless me. Please give life to my husband. I was not at fault. I have been deceived and cheated due to extra love and affection. Widowhood is the heinous curse for a woman."

The Kartika Mata gave a jerk to her and said, "O sinner, leave my feet. O killer of one's own husband leave my feet." But the young widow remained firm and implored her time and again for her husband's life.

At last Kartika Mata became soft and assured her to return her husband's life. She took out "kaajal" from her eyes, Menhdi (myrtle) from her nail, "Roli" from her forehead ornament and sprinkled it with the fore part of the little finger on the dead body.

With Kartika Mata's blessings her husband woke up and said, "O, I had a very-very sound sleep."

The young lady said, "what sort of sleep? I have been serving you for one long year. Chauth Mata has returned life to you."

The young man said, "If it is so let us celebrate this day with festivity." The husband and wife began to play chess game. In the meanwhile the maid servant brought stale food for the young 'widow.' She could not believe her eyes when she saw the young couple playing chess. It was an awful scene for her. She rushed down stairs and informed the old lady. It was a happy news for her.

She hugged the young lady and said, "How life returned to my dear son?" The young lady said, "Chauth Mata has showered blessings upon us." She fell on her mother-in-law's feet.

It was known to one and all on the drum beat to observe Chauth Mata's fast. If possible 13 or 4 or at least 2 "Chauth" fasts, because it gives sight to the eyeless and strength in the knees. It should be celebrated by children's mother and also by those whose husbands are alive. Let bad luck may not visit as it visited the young lady in her early life. Let happiness visit to all as it visited to the young lady in her later life.

The story teller says that one who relates or listens or even nods at this story will remain happy. The unfortunate widowhood will never visit that family.

MARGASHIRSHA

25

HANUMAN PASSES IMPASSABLE

(Sankashta Chaturthi Fast is observed in the name of Ganesha, on the 4th day of the waning moon, in the month of Margashirsha, the 9th month of the Indian Lunar Calendar. Gajanan Ganesha (elephant trunked), an epithet of Ganesha, is worshipped by the devotees. Barley, sesamum, rice and ghee are mixed for using in the "Yajna". It is believed that one can overpower one's enemy by gaining strength through this fast. It bestows all sort of wordly pleasures. Apart from religious belief the story reinforces that blessings are strong pillars to boost mental and physical strength. Elderly advice never goes waste.)

Long-long ago Raja Dashratha ruled over Ayodhya in Tretayuga. He was very fond of hunting. Once unknowingly he shot an arrow on Shravana Kumar, taking him as elephant in darkness, Shravana Kumar's blind parents cursed Dashratha saying that he too would die due to his son's grief. The king was frightened by Brahman's curse.

He arranged "Putreshti Yajna" to obtain male child. As a result Lord Vishnu took birth as his son, later named as Rama, Bhagwati Lakshmi took birth as Sita. Sitaji was married to Rama and she went to jungle with Rama in exile. Rama killed Khar-Dushan and other Rakshashas. Ravana, the king of Lanka, got annoyed and abducted Sita when Rama was out for hunting a golden deer.

Rama left Panchwati where Sitaji was abducted. He marched towards Rishyamooka mountains. He befriended Sugriva who assured Rama for Sita's search out.

Sita's searchout operation was handed over to Angada and Hanuman. Sampati noticed Hanuman's Vanar sena and enquired about their adventure. The Vanaras told him that Vishnu has incarnated as Rama and Lakshmi as Sita. Sitaji has been abducted by some demon and our entire team is searching her out.

Sampati said, "As you serve Rama so we are common friends. I know where Sitaji is. My younger brother Jatayu has sacrificed his life to save and free Sita from Ravana's grip. Demon Ravana lives in Lanka across this sea. He has forcibly taken her away. Sitaji is sitting under a 'seesam' tree and I can still see her."

The Vanar Sena was pleased to hear Sampati. But the question was as to who will go across the sea to confirm Sita's presence and to assure her for her safe recovery.

Angada was too old to jump across the roaring sea. Every body looked towards Hanuman. Sampati said, "O Hanuman, you are the mightiest among all. You can jump across this sea and come back."

Hanuman searched his innerself for a moment and said, "O dear Sampati, how you calculated my strength? I need some one's blessings. Please guide me?"

Sampati smiled and said, "You keep Sankashta Ganesha Chaturthi fast. Lord Ganesha will bless you with additional strength. You will definitely pass across the impassable ocean in the twinkling of an eye. Have faith in Ganesha."

Hanuman adhered to Sampati's advice and took Ganesha Chaturthi fast to restore additional strength. As a result Hanuman succeeded in crossing the ocean and brought back Sitaji's message.

Krishna told Yudhishthira to observe this fast to restore his lost kingdom. Yudhishthira observed this fast and got back his throne with Ganesha's blessings.

PAUSHA

26

GANESHA BLESSED RAVANA

(Ganesha Chaturthi fast is observed on the 4th day of the waning moon in the month of Pausha, the 10th month of the Indian Lunar Calendar. This day is known as "Vighna Vinashini Chaturthi", remover of obstacles. Lambodar Ganesha (pot-bellied Ganesha) is especially worshipped at this occasion. The devotee should remain calm and cool and avoid sleep on this day. He can take Gaumutra (cow's urine) as a drink. If ghee mixed kheer is used for "Havana" even the ruler can be guided according to one's dictates.

The story seems to express that pride hath a fall. Even only one person from the family invites disaster to all relatives.)

Once Ravana, the king of Lanka, conquered all the deities. He was intoxicated due to power. One day, just out of fun, he caught hold of Bali from back side while he was performing Sandhya (uttering prayer). Instinctively he pressed Ravana under his armpit as if it was some toy. Bali flew through sky-way and reached his capital Kishkindha. He made him captive and presented him to his son Angada as a toy.

Angada tied a rope around Ravana's neck and paraded him through the city. The citizens made a horse-laugh when they saw Ravana, once world conquerer, in such a miserable condition. Some of them murmured at his pitiable state.

Ravana felt ashamed and came expirate. His arrogance was crushed. He recalled the name of his maternal grand father, Pulatsya Muni. The Muni was shocked to hear his call. He said to himself, "What act has put him in such a shameful condition. He must be proud of his health and wealth. It is dead sure that pride hath fall,—this or that day—may he be deity, demon or a man.

The Muni reached Kishkindha and met Ravana. Ravana said, "O dear grand sir, my lust for power has put me in my present condition. I caught hold Bali from his back while he was uttering his prayers near Western Ocean, but instead he caught me with full firmness. He brought me here and put a rope around my neck as if I am a toy. The citizens have made fun of me. I feel helpless due to this rope. I am a blot in my lineage. Please protect and help me."

Pulatsya Muni said, "Do not feel afraid. I shall ask the Muni to dischain you. You must remember that Bali belongs to Devaraja Indra's genetics. He is stronger than you. He will be killed by Rama alone. If you want to be free from Bali's trap, you should observe Sankashta Chaturthi's fast in this month i.e., Pausha. Even Lord Indra observed this fast to emancipate him from Vritrasur's murder. You observe this fast and you will be out of this trouble very soon."

After sincere advice the Muni left his "ashrama". Ravana observed this fast and he was freed very soon. Ravana returned to his capital.

Krishna advised Yudhishthira to observe this fast for conquering his enemies and to restore the lost throne. Yudhishthira too observed this fast and regained his lost kingdom.

MAGHA (KRISHNA PAKSHA – I)

27

GANESHA'S MIRACLE IN HARISH CHANDRA'S DAYS

(Ganesha Chaturthi fast is observed on the 4th day of the waning moon, in the month of Magha, the 11th month of the Indian Lunar Calendar. Bhalchandra epithet (moon bearing forehead) of Lord Ganesha is especially worshipped on this day. Sesamum "Laddoos" are offered to the epithet and the devotee too eats them. It is believed that this fast fulfils all desires. It protects children from any untoward accidents.

Apart from religious belief this story seems to reveal that ruler's behaviour is reflected among its subjects and his deed cannot be suppressed for long time. It pricks the sinner. The widowed family needs special care and attention by the ruler.)

King Harishchandra, an illustrious ruler, lived in Satyuga (the first of the four Hindu ages—golden age). He followed Kshatriya Dharma. He was very truthful, skilful and of simple temperament. There was no injustice in his kingdom. There was no handicap, poor or a sufferer at that time. No one experienced mental agony and physical strain. All lived a long and full life.

Rishi Sharma, an ascetic Brahman also lived at that time. Unfortunately he died when he had only one young son. His wife looked after his son. She fed the son by beggary. The lady observed Sankata Chaturthi fast in the month of Magha.

She used to make Ganesha's idol from cowdung for worship. She prepared sesamum laddoo by earning money through begging. Meanwhile her son hang Ganesha's cowdung idol around his neck and went out for play. A satanic ill-willed potter caught hold that five year old boy. He hid him under unbaked pots in his kiln. He put the kiln on fire.

His mother searched her son in every nook and corner but all in vain. She became restless. Wailing and weeping she implored Ganesha. She said, "O plump bodied, bearer of sun like red lustre, wearer of matted hair on the head, please help this aggrieved widow. O elephant mouthed, bearer of four arms, O adorer of moon on the forehead, Vinayaka, the remover of obstacles, master of orphans, granter of boons, I am aggrieved due to my son's disappearance. Please help me, please protect me."

The widowed Brahman lady went on wailing till midnight but all in vain.

On the other hand the potter went to his kiln to unearth the baked pots. To his great surprise he found knee deep water in the kiln when he opened it. To his still great surprise he saw the same boy playing with the unbaked pots. He began to tremble to see that unbelieveable scene. He immediately reported this matter in Harishchandra's court. He also narrated his act of misdeed before the court.

The potter said, "O powerful king, I deserve death for my misdeed. But I too was helpless. I tried to bake pots many times to earn money out of it for my daughter's marriage. Unfortunately all the times the pots remained half baked. I was greatly frightened and approached a "Tantrik" to know some trick. He advised me to sacrifice some boy to attain my goal. I was in a fix. How a person will spare me when he would know about my dreaded design. I exchanged this advice with my wife. As this boy was fatherless I chose a safer course and hid him in my kiln.

Next day I went to my kiln but to my great astonishment, the kiln was under knee deep water and the boy was playing with the pots. I was stunned and so reported the incident to you.

The king was taken aback when he heard that unusual happening. He decided to visit the scene personally. When he saw that scene he said to his minister, "Try to find out the know-how of this boy. Restore the boy to his parents. Also investigate how the kiln was filled with water? How lotus flowers bloom so soon? How 'Vaidurya' coloured green grass grew so soon? Why this boy is safe from fire? How he is not hungry? How he feels here like his own home?"

When the king was raising these probing questions a Brahman woman reached there. She was wailing badly. She began to curse the potter. The old woman's condition was like a cow whose lost calf was sighted back after a long time. She kissed and hugged her son. She sat in the king's feet after restoring consolation.

King Harishchandra said, "O poor old woman, how your son remained safe even in the burning kiln? Do you know some magic or you have performed some religious rites?"

The woman said, "O religious minded king, I do not know any magic nor do I have performed any religious rites. I also do not know about any act regarding penance, Yoga or donation. It is due to the power of Ganesha's fast that my son has been spared." The king was pleased to hear old woman's simplicity and unshakeable faith. The king made a 'parikrama' (a going around an idol or respectable person as a mark of reverence) around the lady. He also announced that all his subjects should observe this fast onward.

According to the story teller this story was first related to Parvati by Shiva. Later on, the same story was repeated by Ganesha to Parvati. In the present context Krishna is relating this story to Yudhishthira. Yudhishthira observed this fast to regain his lost kingdom and later on succeeded in his goal.

MAGHA (KRISHNA PAKSHA – II)

28

GANESHA CHAUTH

(The present story is a good example as how a selfish and miser person breaks his or her words. It also reflects how one is heavily punished for this sin. If one commits a sin others also have to bear the brunt.)

There was a rich businessman couple. They never observed any religious rites. They took them as useless acts. Once her neighbour, an old lady, was relating the story of "Maghi Chauth" (4th day falling in the month of Magha, the 10th month of Lunar Calendar.) The rich lady went to her and said, "What are you doing today?"

The old lady said, "I am performing 'Maghi Chauth' fast's ceremony."

"What is it meant for?" The rich lady asked.

The old lady said, "This fast bestows wealth and progeny."

The rich lady was happy to know because she was issueless. She said, "If I am conceived, this month I shall observe this fast and donate one and a quarter seer of 'Tilkuti'" (sweet cake prepared from sesamum seeds).

Fortunately she became pregnant. She took it in a light way and said, "Oh Chauth Mata, I shall donate two and a half seer of 'Tilkuti' if and when I deliver a son."

After nine months she delivered a son. She was very miser. She said, "Oh Chauth Mata, I shall donate one and quarter maund of "Tilkuti" at the time of my son's marriage."

As the time passed on she arranged her son's marriage and fixed the date for the same. The Chauth Mata and Ganesha exchanged their views. Chauth Mata said, "This rich lady is very strange. She promised to donate Tilkuti if she is conceived. Next, she promised to donate it after her delivery. Now she has arranged her son's marriage. She must be taught a lesson. If we do no show our might and worth who will have faith in us in this Kalyuga?" They planned to abduct the bridegroom right at the time of marriage ceremony.

The bride and bridegroom were sitting around the holy fire to complete marriage ceremony. When they had taken three rounds the bridegroom was abducted from the scene. The whole environment of gay and enjoyment became gloomy. The "Baratis" searched here and there but could not trace him. The bride's family could not express their grief out of shocking experience. They were thinking themselves guilty because they could not protect the bridegroom. The Barat returned empty handed without bride and bridegroom.

Ganesha and Chauth Mata placed the bridegroom over a "peepal" tree. The girls from the village went to the jungle to worship Gangaur and to collect fodder. They noted a strange shadow in the tree. It was resounding some sound. None of them could make out any meaning out of that happening.

Once the "half-wed" bride happened to pass that way. She heard a sound which said, "O my half-wed bride, come to me, come to me."

She was horrified to hear that call. One day her mother said, "My dear daughter, I give you best food to eat. Why are you becoming weaker and weaker every day? Does some spirit haunts you."

The girl wept. Her mother consoled her and insisted on telling the truth. The girl gained some confidence and said, "Whenever I pass through that "peepal" tree I hear a call. It says—O my half-wed bride, come to me, come to me. In a shady look I note a young man dressed in a wedding robe. He wears a wedding crown."

Her mother said, "O dear daughter, please take me to him. He may be your bridegroom."

The girl led her to that "peepal" tree. The young man repeated his old call. Her mother recognised him and said,

"Why do not you marry my daughter? What forced you to leave the holy marriage fire? Please tell me the truth."

The young man addressed her from the "peepal" tree, "I am under the siege of Ganesha and Chauth Mata. I cannot say anything more. Better you contact my mother. She may tell you the reason."

The old lady went to the bridegroom's mother and said "Did you ever give some commitment in the name of Ganesha or Chauth Mata? They have sieged your son."

The old lady recollected and said, "Yes, yes, first I committed one and a quarter seer of 'Tilkuti' before his birth. Then I committed two and a half seer 'Tilkuti' and later on one and a quarter maund 'Tilkuti' at the time of his marriage. But I never fulfilled my words. Ganesha and Chauth Mata must have punished me for my non commitment."

After expressing deep sorrow and repentance the rich lady said, "If my son returns I shall distribute two and a half maund of 'Tilkuti.' The bride's mother said, "I shall distribute two and a quarter maund of 'Tilkuti' if my son-in-law is freed by Ganesha and Chauth mata."

Ganesha and Chauth Mata were satisfied with the commitment of both the ladies because as a punishment they were paying many a times than they committed earlier. They freed the bridegroom. He came down the tree and reached the bride's home.

The remaining marriage ceremony was rearranged and every body felt happy on the extraordinary reunion. All the members of both the families observed Chauth Mata's fast and distributed "Tilkuti" in the neighbouring area.

The story teller says—let all newly wed couple, if separated, meet again like this couple. Let happiness prevail in those families where this story is related and listened too. Let a person who nods during listening this story may get happiness.

29

HERAMBA GANESHA'S BENEFICTIONS

(Ganesha Chaturthi fast is observed on the 4th day of the waning moon, in the month of Phalguna, the 12th month of the Indian Lunar Calendar. The epithet of Heramba (one who always remembers Shiva) is especially worshipped on this day. The devotees take ghee and sugar as a diet. A special "Havan" is performed with mixing "kheer" and "kaner" (oleander).

It seems that this story is a tribute to the ageing person who deserves family regard and respect. Those are blessed who give due respect to the elderman of the family. It is not the large size but the well-knit family which is an ideal one.)

In good olden days there ruled a king named Yuvanashva. He was religious minded, liberal, charitable and gave respect to the deities and Brahmans. In those days there lived a Brahman. His name was Vishnu Sharma. He was a great scholar of the Vedanta and other scriptures. He had seven sons. They were all well off. But all of them were always at loggerhead and established separate homes.

Vishnu Sharma took his meal with each son by rotation. He grew old and weak. All of her daughter-in-laws disrespected him. He lived a humiliated life.

One day Vishnu Sharma observed Ganesha Chaturthi fast and went to the eldest daughter-in-law. He said, "O dear daughter-in-law, today I have observed Ganesha Chaturthi fast. Please arrange my meals and other articles needed for the fast. Ganesha will be pleased with us and you would become wealthy."

The daughter-in-law said in very disrespectful tone, "I have no spare time for you. I cannot bear this disturbance. You always play a game under this or that pretext. Today it is in the name of Ganesha. I do not know anything about Ganesha or the fast related to it. Please slip away from my house."

Having been rebuked by the eldest daughter-in-law he knocked the doors of all other five sons but received the same fate. Badly humiliated he went to the youngest daughter-in-law and repeated the same words. She said, "Why do you feel so sad and dismay. You observe this fast as you please. I shall also observe this fast. We shall be freed from all day-to-day troubles."

After assuring her father-in-law she went for begging the needed articles. She arranged "laddoos" for him. She also stored sandalwood, flowers, dhoop, rice, fruit, earthen lamp, Naivedya (food to be offered to gods) and betel-leaf. She arranged them systematically and joined her father-in-law in worshipping ceremony. She offered him food with due regards and respect. She could not arrange food for herself and remained hungry.

At midnight the old man suffered from loose motions and vomitting. Both of his legs were sprinked with the release. She washed his feet and cleaned his body. She cursed herself because she could not pay full attention to him due to her fast. She wept throughout night and unknowingly it was "jaagran" (to pass night without sleep and uttering prayers) for her. The day light broke. She was surprised to see heaps of diamonds, jewels and other precious stones in her house. The rooms were dazzling with these stones. Her father-in-law had restored full health by that time.

She said to her father-in-law, "Whose property is this? How this house has been stuffed with this wealth? Is it some conspiracy to entrap us in theft case?"

The old man smiled and said, "O good natured lady, your behaviour towards elders and unshakeable faith has borne fruit. Lord Ganesha has bestowed it upon you."

The daughter-in-law said, "I do not want to take this credit. It goes to you because I observed this fast for your sympathy. Our poverty has gone due to your tolerant behaviour and faith in Ganesha."

When the other ladies came to know about her richness they became furious and were enraged. They said, "It is impartiality. The old man has given all hidden treasure to the youngest lady."

To pacify the storm of jealousy the old man clarified that he had nothing to do with that wealth. It did not belong to him. Lord Ganesha bestowed this wealth to the youngest lady due to Ganesha Chaturthi fast. He further said, "I requested you all to help me in performing this fast. All of you rebuked me under this or that pretext. The youngest lady arranged necessary articles for fast. Even she had to beg for them. All these riches belong to her."

All the ladies realised their mistake. They begged pardon from the oldman and started observing Ganesha Chaturthi's fast. Later on they also became rich.

The story teller says that Krishna related this story to Yudhishthira and advised him to observe this fast to regain the lost glory. Yudhishthira followed Krishna's advice and regained his lost kingdom.

30
RAJA CHANDER SEN AND GANESHA

(A special Ganesha Chaturthi Katha (story) is related on the 4th day of the waning moon of this month i.e., Leap year.* It seems that the aim of this story is manifold. Firstly, it repeats the rituals expected to be observed on fast's days. Secondly, it repeats the importance and worldly gains of this fast. Thirdly, the story reflects other dimensions. They can be enumerated as under—kingship is not for ever. It can be attained through pious acts and lost through negligence. Good or bad deeds pass on to the next birth. The lives of Rishis and Munis is for others. Their preachings and sayings are neutral. Likewise worldly happiness and pains are like light and shadow. One should not think oneself supreme but pay obedience before supreme power. This power can be in the form of incarnated personalities, deities, celestial spirits, Rishi Munis or elderly persons.)

Once Shiva was sitting among Rishis. He was in a happy mood. When asked by Rishis he said, "I shall relate you an auspicious story. It will reveal the greatness of Ganesha Chaturthi's fast.

---

*(Indian Lunar Calendar i.e., Vikram Samvat, has twelve months. After every four years falls an extra month, called "Adhik masa", "Londmasa" or "Mala masa" or leap year. It can be any lunar month but generally it is in hot season when rotating land expands due to heat and takes extra time in rotation. It is believed that during this month Lord Vishnu rests in the Ocean. The devotees spend this month in Bhajan-Kirtan and organise special kathas.)

"When Pandavas were in exile they always adored Krishna day in and day out. Once, while strolling, Vyasa visited their cottage at his own will. All of them welcomed him with folded hands. They said, "We have been blessed by your kind presence and so is our cottage. Your pious feet have blest our lives. We feel as if we have attained all success because your presence deters all sorrows. We give you a hearty welcome. Though deprived from our kingdom, still we thank our stars by seeing you personally. With these welcome words all the Pandavas—Arjuna, Bhima, Nakula, Sahdeva and Yudhishthira again bowed before him. Draupadi offered Paadya (water for washing elder's feet), Arghya (presents), Aachman (rinsing water to be used before ceremony) and Aasan (mat) to the Rishi.

After paying due courtesy Draupadi said, "O Muni, I even being a queen was insulted in Duryodhan's full bench court through dragging hair. Later on I was exiled. What should I do to free myself from all the troubles and to defeat our enemies?" Yudhishthira also proposed the same question.

The omniscient Muni replied very kindly, "O Yudhisthira, you are the most religious person upon this earth. There is no match for you. I shall tell you such a pious fast which will remove your troubles. This fast is auspicious and will bear fruit. It is celestial and washes away all wordly worries. The students attain knowledge and those who desire wealth are bestowed with it. I shall relate you an old legend connected with this fast.

In olden days in Satyuga, there lived a king named Chander Sen. He enunciated himself in a cult and lived with his wife, children and other members of his family. Fortunately, his wife was skilful and faithful. Her name was Ratnavati. They were in great love with each other.

As the misfortune would had it they were deprived of their kingdom by the enemy. They occupied their treasures and army also. Even the king was deserted by his relatives.

Having been deprived of his kingdom he went to the jungles with his wife. They were hungry and thirsty due to duress. They had only one cloth with them. They tumbled throughout the way. By sunset they reached a place which was infested with lions, tigers, ruddy goose, hersans, storks and koyals. A thorn got stuck into the queen's foot. The king shared her pain.

In the morning they saw Markandeya Rishi. They approached him with great difficulty due to hunger, thirst and tiredness. They paid him obedience by lying down on the ground. Some other pious persons also gathered there.

The king stood up before the holy gathering and said, "O most respectful Rishi, I have a doubt in my mind. Please console me by your seasoned answer. What sort of sin I committed in my previous life which deprived me from my kingdom and power?"

Markandeya Rishi said, "O king, listen the story about your previous birth. I reveal it before you. . . .

Once you went out for hunting in deep jungles. While hunting deer, leopards and rabbits, it was dark night. Incidentally that was the 4th day of waning moon, in the leap month of the lunar year. You spotted a beautiful pond. You were surprised to see red saree clad "nagakanyas" (a beautiful female race of semi-divine beings). All of them were worshipping Ganesha. You approached them and said respect fully, "O heavenly nymphs, please tell me how to worship Ganesha. What is the effect of this worship, because I want to worship him."

Nagakanyas said, "You must worship Ganesha. It bestows all siddhis or accomplishments. It gives eternal peace, thriving strength, happiness, progeny and wealth."

The king said, "O Nagakanyas, in which month and on what dates I perform this worship? what articles are to be donated? What is it's ceremonial order? Please answer my questions one by one."

The Nagakanyas said, "O king of kings, worship Ganesha after seeing the moonrise on the 4th day of the waning moon, in the month of leap year. The devotee should offer 'Puja' according to his own capacity. Offer bath to Ganesha with 'Panchamrit' (mixture consisting of milk, curd, sugar, honey and ghee.) Offer red cloth to its idol. Also offer 'Gandha' (Scent), Dhoop (incence), Deep (earthen lamp), Naivedhya (oblation), Durva (green grass), Vastra (pair of cloth) and Sugandhit Dravya (scented objects). Prepare fifteen 'laddoos' as food to be offered to the idol. Distribute five 'laddoos' each to Ganesha, Brahman and to unmarried girls and break the fast. Listen to Ganesha Katha as described in the Puranas. This will fulfil devotee's desires and he will attain Siddhi. This is the procedure for Ganesha worship."

The king thanked Nagakanyas and paid due reverence before departure. He took a solemn promise to observe that fast. He meditated Ganesha for some time on the bank of the pond and returned home.

Markandeya said, "As Ganesha was pleased with you, he bestowed beautiful wife, son, wealth and what not. Your palace was filled with diamonds, jewels, cows, horses and elephants. But after some time you became proud of your worldly possessions and forgot to observe fast.

"After some time you met your death. As you worshipped Ganesha you took birth in a royal family and enjoyed all worldly pleasure. Due to false pride and breaking your promise you are facing all these troubles."

The king said, "O Rishi, please give me proper guidance for regaining my old glory."

Markandeya said, "You worship Ganesha as per direction given before and observe fast."

Vyasa said that the king took solemn oath and went back. He took fast along with the queen with full faith. Due to Ganesha's kind grace he overpowered his enemies and regained his lost glory.

Yudhishthira listened this story with full attention and said, "O respected Vyasa, please tell me the proper way for worshipping Ganesha."

Vyasa explained with full details and Yudhishthira worshipped Ganesha properly. He observed fast also. As a result he defeated all of his enemies in the warfield and ruled over Bharat Varsha for many years.